Reading this book is like sitting on the couch [with a thera]pist. In *Are You Really OK?* Debra shows u[s how our] emotional, and mental health are intertwined [...] professional experience. The book is full of wisdom, understanding, and practical tools that will make a difference in your life today.

—*Christine Caine,* founder of A21 and Propel Women

A great book that invites the reader to delve into a more abundant life of spiritual, emotional, mental, and physical health. You'll be challenged and equipped to grow, mature, and spiritually prosper. Marvelously done!

—*Gary Thomas,* author of *Sacred Marriage*

Every one of us has been damaged by others, has damaged others, and has damaged ourselves by unwise words and unhealthy actions. As a result, we all have hurts, hang-ups, and bad habits. So where do we go to get help? In her newest book, *Are You Really OK?*, Debra is your personal counselor and life coach who shares openly about her journey toward health and makes clear next steps for you to take toward personal healing.

—*Chris Reed,* pastor at Saddleback Church

I am thrilled Debra has written such a helpful resource that unpacks what it looks like to pursue emotional, spiritual, mental, and physical health. In a culture that often presents a skewed version of health, this topic has never been more important. If you want to grow, this is for you!

—*Ben Stuart,* pastor of Passion City Church DC and author of *Single, Dating, Engaged, Married*

I cannot emphasize enough how important this book is. Debra is an excellent counselor, and in the pages ahead she will take you on a journey toward emotional, spiritual, mental, and physical health. You are going to learn new things, you are going to change in the best ways, and you are going to enjoy every word.

—*Jonathan Pokluda,* bestselling author of *Welcome to Adulting* and pastor of Harris Creek Baptist Church

Are You Really OK? sets a new standard for how mental health is handled in the church. Debra gives such practical steps not just to heal but thrive! I'm so thankful for her work and getting this message out. It's a must read.

—*Caitlin Zick*, Moral Revolution codirector and author of *Look at You, Girl*

If you are worn-out from years of faking fine and are ready to address some hard truths, Debra Fileta wants to help. In her new book, *Are You Really OK?*, Debra offers her life experience, her psychology background, and her love for people and captures it in a resource that will help you live an honest, holistic, and healthy life. Debra is a master at professionally guiding others through the process of an in-depth assessment of themselves. In this book, she will do the same for you. You can be more than "just okay," and Debra Fileta will show you how.

—*Chrystal Evans Hurst*, bestselling author and speaker

ARE YOU REALLY OK?

DEBRA FILETA

M.A., LPC

HARVEST HOUSE PUBLISHERS
EUGENE, OREGON

Cover by Faceout Studio
Interior design by Angie Renich / Wildwood Digital Publishing
Cover image © kjohanse / Gettyimages

For bulk, special sales, or ministry purchases, please call 1-800-547-8979.
Email: Customerservice@hhpbooks.com

 is a federally registered trademark of the Hawkins Children's LLC. Harvest House Publishers, Inc., is the exclusive licensee of the trademark.

Are You Really OK?

Copyright © 2021 by Debra Fileta
Published by Harvest House Publishers
Eugene, Oregon 97408
www.harvesthousepublishers.com

ISBN 978-0-7369-8251-1 (pbk.)
ISBN 978-0-7369-8252-8 (eBook)
ISBN 978-0-7369-8544-4 (eAudio)

Library of Congress Cataloging-in-Publication Data

Names: Fileta, Debra K., author.
Title: Are you really OK? / Debra Fileta.
Description: Eugene, Oregon : Harvest House Publishers, [2021] | Includes
    bibliographical references. | Summary: "Pursuing the spiritual,
    emotional, mental, and physical health God desires for you is a lifelong
    commitment that requires honest self-examination and intentional living.
    In Are You Really OK? author and licensed counselor Debra Fileta will
    help you take inventory of yourself so you can recognize where you need
    growth and healing"—Provided by publisher.
Identifiers: LCCN 2020052739 (print) | LCCN 2020052740 (ebook) | ISBN
    9780736982511 (trade paperback) | ISBN 9780736982528 (ebook)
Subjects: LCSH: Mental health—Religious aspects—Christianity. | Mind and
    body—Religious aspects—Christianity.
Classification: LCC BT732.4 .F55 2021 (print) | LCC BT732.4 (ebook) | DDC
    248.8/62—dc23
LC record available at https://lccn.loc.gov/2020052739
LC ebook record available at https://lccn.loc.gov/2020052740

Printed in the United States of America

23 24 25 26 27 28 / BP-AR / 10 9 8

This book is dedicated to every single person who has invited me into their lives on their journey of healing. Being entrusted with your stories is a deep honor and a great responsibility. What a privilege to watch the Lord restore all of the broken places as we travel on this road toward healing together.

And to you, reading this book. Thank you for entrusting me with your journey. May God bring the healing that only He can bring through every page and every chapter.

CONTENTS

Foreword by Levi Lusko   9

Introduction: You're Not as Healthy As You Think You Are 13

Part 1: Emotional Health

1. Going Underneath the Surface: Emotional Awareness 23

2. Patterns Lead to Process: Emotional History 47

3. God Is More Real than My Reality: Emotional Control 69

Part 2: Spiritual Health

4. God Is _____: My View of God 97

5. Hello, My Name Is _____: My View of Self 113

6. Significant Others: My View of Relationships 127

Part 3: Mental Health

7. What's on Repeat? Cognitive Distortions 145

8. Anxiety, Depression, and the Church:
   Mental Health Matters 159

9. Trauma Messes with Your Head: Peeling Back the Layers 179

Part 4: Physical Health

10. Back to the Basics: The Body-Mind Connection 203

11. Stop Living on Empty: The Art of Self-Care 215

12. Time Doesn't Heal All Wounds: One Year from Today 231

Notes 247

FOREWORD
Levi Lusko

The sky was streaked with oranges and pinks and purples. The reflection of those colors into the turquoise lake caused a surreal tie-dye effect that amplified the sunset. You could hardly tell where the sky ended and the water began. Everything was glowing.

My daughters and son and I were standing on a dock fishing and taking it all in. It felt as though we were in the middle of a painting. Soon the stars would come out and we would retreat to our campfire for s'mores. This was Montana summer majesty at its absolute finest. We were having so much fun that even when the sun finally set, we lit a lantern and stayed on the dock while the kids kept casting their bait-laden hooks into the water.

At one point my daughter Daisy said, "Dad, I think I have a bite!" And so I leaped to her side and encouraged her to steadily reel the fish in.

As she spun the little crank, I heard the sound a pole makes when the fish is too big—the reel stops gathering line to avoid breaking the string. "You must have snagged a monster!" I said. I adjusted the drag a little bit as she continued to faithfully fight this sea monster. And nothing changed. The reel just continued to make that unmistakable clicking sound and kept the line in place.

It was at that point that I looked up and realized that her pole wasn't bent at all, which it would have been if there were a fish on the line. I realized what had happened when my eyes made it to the tip of her pole. There was her hook and little sinker right at the top. She hadn't caught a fish at all. She felt all the tension because she had reached the end of her line.

I wonder if you can relate.

I know I can.

To be human is to have a line that is finite. There is a limit to every one of our abilities, and there is only so much we can take. This is as true mentally and emotionally as it is physically and spiritually. Maybe, like Daisy, you're feeling that no matter how much you spin your wheels, you just aren't gaining traction. So you struggle with stress and worry, anxiousness or dread. The answer isn't to just try harder. Muscle can't win this battle.

As the saying goes, "Insanity is doing the same thing over and over and expecting different results." Simply put, keep doing what you've always done and you'll keep getting what you've always got. The tension you are feeling is telling you that you have reached the end of your line.

This masterful book will help you get your hook back in the water.

Debra Fileta will help you understand who you are—the full you: body, soul, mind, and heart. And like a chair that works only when all four legs are firmly planted on the ground, the truths she will share will help you figure out which of your "legs" is shorter than the others and needs to be propped up. It doesn't really work to focus all your attention on your spiritual life when your physical or emotional health is a mess. Like the beautiful sunset we watched that night in which all the colors blended together, your life is meant to be a vibrant reflection of every facet of your life. This isn't possible if you ignore entire components of your well-being.

In the church we can be guilty of looking for spiritual solutions to physical or emotional problems. You might not have a demon—you might just be dehydrated. Prayer is important, but so is counseling. And while no one would ever tell a person with poor vision to correct their eyesight with Bible verses—we'd advise them to get prescription lenses!—there can be a stigma around a similar prescription for treating a chemical deficiency. Debra helps us avoid such narrow thinking and unhelpful dichotomies. It's not either/or, but both/and. Prayer is important and so is counseling. Being in a small group at church is vital, and depending on what you are walking through, medicine might be too.

There is an old adage about the cobbler who had no shoes. It can be easy to not do for yourself what you do for a living. My favorite thing about this book is how it defies that stereotype. Debra is honest about her own struggles and transparent about her journey to implement the practices that, as a professional counselor, she advocates for you and me to do. I hope and pray that as you embark upon this journey, you will open your heart, soul, mind, and strength to all that Jesus wants to do in you. I am confident that greater joy and peace are waiting on the other side.

INTRODUCTION

You're Not as Healthy As You Think You Are

You're not as healthy as you think you are.

That's a presumptuous sentence for the start of a book, but if you've continued reading to sentence two even after reading sentence one, then you're exactly the kind of person I want to be reading along. Because the conversations that we're about to have throughout the chapters of this book need to be had with people who are not easily offended. They need to be had with people who are ready to reflect, to question, to grow. People who aren't afraid to be challenged or pushed out of their comfort zone. People who are ready to redefine their view of themselves and who God has made them to be. People who are ready to face the hard questions and dig deep to answer: Are you *really* okay?

And if you've made it this far, you're likely that kind of person. You're ready. I can just feel it. You're ready to stop being content with the skewed version of health that has rubbed off on us from this culture— the version that can look so good on the outside yet fail to actually deal with what's happening on the inside. The version that has gotten so good at presenting its picture-perfect self on Instagram yet fails to acknowledge its flaws and struggles and failures. The version that presents the façade that everything is fine, when really, everything is not. I'm beyond ready to stop playing this game and to acknowledge that just because we're Christian doesn't mean we're healthy. No, not even close.

According to a long line of psychological studies, we humans have a tendency to see ourselves as better than we are. Social scientists call this the better-than-average-effect.[1] When asked how well they drive, how good of a friend they are, or how morally they behave, the majority of people will rate themselves as better than the average. Mathematically speaking, this can't be the reality—half of all people will fall below the median. So, not only do people think of themselves as better than average, but they think better of themselves than they actually should. In other words, they think they're doing okay when, in fact, they might not be.

It was hypothesized that people view themselves as above average only when they're higher in socioeconomic status or only in certain groups that actually are above average in certain areas, so another study was performed to test the effect on a group of prisoners. Prisoners were asked to assess their view of themselves with regard to their kindness and morality, comparing themselves to nonprisoners in their personal assessment. Sure enough, the prisoners affirmed the better-than-average effect shows no bias: They saw themselves as above average in both kindness and morality in comparison to nonprisoners.[2] It doesn't matter if you're a pastor or a prisoner because according to human nature, you likely think of yourself as better than you actually are. And this applies to every area of our life. It applies to our actions and choices, our feelings and emotions, our behaviors and interactions, our thoughts and ideas, and everything in between. Just because we're Christians doesn't mean we're healthy. And just because we think we're doing okay doesn't mean we really are.

> It doesn't matter if you're a pastor or a prisoner because according to human nature, you likely think of yourself as better than you actually are.

We live in a culture that has set us up to put our best face forward. A culture that deceives us into believing that the better we appear, the better we are. But just because we seem to have it together on the outside doesn't mean that we have it together on the inside. And just because we've come to Jesus at some point in our journey doesn't mean we've magically achieved perfection. We need to stop *assuming* health and start *pursuing* health, living intentionally toward health on every level.

> We need to stop *assuming* health and start *pursuing* health, living intentionally toward health on every level.

Heart, Soul, Mind, Strength

In the book of Mark, Jesus was asked to explain what the greatest commandment was out of all the commandments. Jesus answered, "The most important one...is this: 'Hear, O Israel: The Lord our God, the Lord is one. Love the Lord your God with all your heart and with all your soul and with all your mind and with all your strength'" (Mark 12:29-30). One thing I love about His direct answer is that it covers every single base. Loving God is not just something we do in our hearts. Loving God is something we have to do with every layer of who we are: with our emotions, our spirit, our thoughts, and our body. Loving God is a holistic experience. It requires every part of who we are to be in alignment with every part of who He is.

As Christians, we have a tendency to put all our focus on loving God with our spirit. We have spiritual conversations, we hear spiritual messages, we sing spiritual songs, and we read spiritual books. We can get so focused on our time in God's Word, our prayer life, and our weekly church gatherings that we fail to take inventory of the health of every other part of our lives. What about our emotional health? What about our mental health? And what about our physical health? Are we making space in our lives for these important considerations? Because if we're not loving God with all of those aspects of ourselves, can we say that we're loving Him well? If we're struggling in one or two of those areas, could that struggle be impacting the rest?

I always say that healthy people make healthy relationships, but you know what? The reverse is also true. Unhealthy people make unhealthy relationships.

Coming to Jesus Doesn't Fix Everything

In the church culture we've created, we falsely assume that coming to Jesus fixes everything. Maybe we don't actually say those words out loud, but we have this latent belief that we're going to have it together emotionally, spiritually, and mentally just because we're walking with the Lord. Yet we don't apply that mentality to our bodies, do we? We don't assume that just because we come to Jesus, all of a sudden we're going to have just the right BMI, our blood pressure will be just right, and all of our physical flaws will disappear.

> Loving God is a holistic experience. It requires every part of who we are to be in alignment with every part of who He is.

My friend Pastor Levi Lusko affirmed this when I visited Fresh Life Church: "We don't get a six pack when we get saved or biceps when we get baptized." We'd never make that crazy assumption with our physical health, and we often do the work that needs to be done to meet our physical health goals. But then why do we make that assumption with regard to our emotional and mental health? Why do we fail to get educated and set goals from the inside out? Why do we so severely neglect taking inventory of what is actually going on inside of us?

Taking Inventory of Heart, Soul, Mind, and Strength

If we're to love God with all our heart, soul, mind, and strength, we need to align ourselves with His best for us in all these areas. Taking inventory of each of those areas is of vital importance, and that's the work we'll be doing throughout the chapters of this book. Chapter by chapter, page by page, we're going to take the time to dig deep and ask ourselves how we're really doing in our emotional, spiritual, mental, and physical health. We're going to start living intentionally toward health, and not just assuming we're okay.

That doesn't mean we're ever going to reach perfection, but we do need to have a proper perspective of who we are versus who God has called us to be. We need to see the gap between our flesh and God's Spirit and do whatever is in our power to move in His direction. Our personal health and development impacts absolutely *everything*. It impacts the quality of our life, it impacts our relationships, it impacts our marriages, it impacts our families, it impacts our ministries, and most importantly, it impacts our callings. We need to be strengthened and empowered to do what God has called us to do with no hindrance.

> The journey to health is about the small steps we take each and every day. Those steps create the roads that shape the maps of our lives.

How often have we seen Christians in the media fall from the height of leadership and into sin and struggle? How often do we see seemingly strong people wreck their marriages and their families and their ministries because they've chosen adultery or addictions? How many more suicides, how much more drug abuse or alcoholism do we need to see before we realize that maybe we ourselves are susceptible to sin and struggle?

Going from unhealth to health is a journey, just as going from health back to unhealth is a journey. It doesn't happen overnight. It's all about the small steps we take each and every day. Those steps create the roads that shape the maps of our lives. We don't go from 0 to 100 in a day. And that's good news for all of us because if we can't go from 0 to 100 in a day, then we also can't go from 100 to 0 in a day. The journey toward health is slow, steady, and stable. It takes our unrelenting awareness and our unhindered intention to do the next right thing, after the next right thing, after the next right thing. We do what we can do, and trust God to continue doing the rest.

God has been lighting a fire in my bones lately regarding the message of personal health among Christians and the importance of coming to terms with who we are and how we're really doing mentally, emotionally, spiritually, and physically. But just recently, this fire got to a place where it singed me. Sometimes the very thing you are passionate about is the very thing that ends up causing you the most pain. Because usually, our passion is birthed out of our pain. That statement was beyond true for me one recent summer as I found myself walking through a level of anxiety and depression and physical illness that I've never experienced before. I have so much more to share about this life-altering experience through the chapters of this book, but I want you to know that being a licensed professional counselor doesn't make me immune to emotional and mental distress, just like being a pastor doesn't make you immune to spiritual attack, or being a doctor doesn't make you immune to physical illness.

> We shouldn't be surprised by the struggle. Instead, we should be prepared!

If we are to love God with all our heart, soul, mind, and strength, then it makes sense that the enemy—the father of lies and destruction—would do whatever he can to ensure that we face struggle in our heart, soul, mind, and strength (John 8:44). The core areas in which you are to love God are the core areas that are susceptible to struggle. We shouldn't be surprised by the struggle. Instead, we should be prepared! The enemy is going to use whatever he can to get us down and out, but by God's power and through His strength, we have what it takes to face those struggles and come out stronger on the other side— mentally, emotionally, spiritually, and physically in Jesus's name.

Coming to Jesus doesn't fix everything. It doesn't fix our high cholesterol levels, and it doesn't fix our lonely childhoods, and it doesn't fix our proclivities toward fear and anxiety. That fix will only come when the trumpet sounds and when all things are made new. But in the meantime, in this life, the Spirit gives us what we need to come face-to-face with our struggles and declare that *Christ will be victorious in the end* (1 Corinthians 15:57)!

Over the course of the next 12 chapters, we are going to dive deep into every aspect of personal health. We're going to talk about preparing your heart, your soul, your mind, and your strength. We're going to take inventory of your emotional, spiritual, mental, and physical health. We're going to ask the hard questions and face the raw answers because we're ready to stop pretending that just because we're Christians means we have it all together. We're ready to begin bridging the gap between who we actually are and who God has called us to be. We're ready to live intentionally toward emotional, spiritual, mental, and physical health.

I know you're ready too. You're exactly the kind of person I want to come with me, and I'm honored to be taking this journey by your side. So, here we go. Let's do this.

PART 1

Emotional Health

Getting Real with Your Heart

Love the Lord your God with all your heart.

LUKE 10:27

1

Going Underneath the Surface

Emotional Awareness

The last place I would have ever expected to have a panic attack was on a safari bus.

I'd studied all about panic attacks, and I'd worked with countless people who'd experienced them. It was part of my job to help people navigate through feelings of anxiety, depression, guilt, shame, and everything in between, and to be candid, I was pretty good at it. I had read all the books and knew all the strategies (or so I thought). But it's one thing to know about emotional struggles and a whole other thing to experience emotional struggles.

It was a hot, 96-degree day in September. Labor Day weekend would be a perfect time to take the kids to a local safari experience that we had on our bucket list. We got to the park and walked around for a while until we realized it was too hot to keep walking. The safari tour bus was leaving in a few minutes, so we decided to get our tickets and head toward the line. I remember thinking how hot it was, noticing the significant amount of sweat we were dripping, and reminding the kids to make sure they were staying hydrated. We bought a couple bottles of water and got in line. Within a few moments, the safari bus pulled up in its animal print colors of black and bright orange. It was a rugged bus, with huge wheels and no roof so you could reach out and feed the wild animals as you took a tour through the "wilderness."

We hopped on the bus and got settled, and within moments our group had entered a mock-up of the African savannah. There were elk, deer, water buffalo, and bison to begin with. Then we drove by some giraffes and eventually into a large herd of Watusi (an African breed of cattle with gigantic horns). The bus stopped to give the cattle a chance to get close and to give the riders an opportunity to feed them as they passed by.

All of a sudden, I became very aware of my body. My focus went from looking at the things around me to feeling what was going on inside of me. I realized how hot my head was feeling with the sun beating down on my black head of hair. The next thing you know, I started sweating profusely. My mouth felt dry, and I felt a tingling going up each of my hands all the way up to the top of my arms. My heart rate started climbing, and I could hear my pulse like the sound of a deafening drum beating in my ear. I felt like I was breathing through a tiny straw.

And then I started panicking. *What is wrong with me? Am I about to pass out on this safari bus?* My thoughts began to spiral. *There's nowhere to go! What do I do? I can't get off this bus right now! There are animals with huge horns everywhere, and I'm completely stuck!* My brain was spinning with silent thoughts, and I was plummeting down, down, down, down and feeling worse and worse with each passing second. I couldn't control what was happening in my body. I felt helpless. I felt scared. I felt desperate. I wanted to scream and run, I wanted to tell the bus driver to get me off this bus, but there was nowhere to go.

My six-year-old son, who was sitting next to me on the bus, broke my distressed thoughts with his whining. "Mom, I'm hot," he said as he grabbed the bottle of water I was clutching in my hands without even realizing it. He took a drink and handed me the water bottle, and I guzzled it down as fast as I could. It helped a little, and my spiraling thoughts began to slow. I was completely out of control, but no one else around me seemed to notice. Not my son sitting next to me, nor my husband and kids sitting in front of me, nor any of the people around me.

Eventually, the tingling in my arms stopped, and my breathing and heart rate came back to normal. This whole experience probably took all of three minutes, but it felt like an eternity. There was a moment in those few minutes that I truly thought I was going to die. But now, somehow, I felt like things were starting to settle. I made it through the rest of the bus ride, although I was definitely on high alert. When we got off the bus, I pulled my husband aside and told him what had just happened.

"I'm so sorry you went through that, babe!" he said. "Why didn't you tell me?"

I thought about his question for a moment and realized that I didn't tell him because I didn't even know what was happening in the moment. I thought my body was failing me. I wondered if I was going to pass out or die. But really, my emotions had taken control.

Really, I had experienced my first panic attack.

Roots Run Deep

I had always been somewhat of an anxious child growing up. I have so many memories and experiences of dealing with feelings of fear and worry that, looking back, I see glaringly how far back the roots of my sensing emotions can be traced.

Somewhere along the way, my mind had absorbed the worries I'd heard about in the world around me. Most children can hear about things like a house fire in the neighborhood or a robbery on the news, worry about it for a few moments, and then shrug it off. But sensitive children sense things more than other children; they have a tendency to hold on to those worries and to absorb them as their own. So, I became one of those kids that couldn't go to sleep without a specific routine. Before saying goodnight, I'd walk around the house and make sure that all the plugs were fastened into the electrical outlets properly and the doors were locked and secured. I had to make sure no fires would start and no robbers would break and enter as we slept.

I even had a routine to follow when it came to saying goodnight. My brother's room was across the hall, and every night before bed I thought of all the things I wanted to tell him just in case this was our last night together. At church, I learned about the rapture and how Jesus would come like a thief in the night, so I just wanted to make sure I made my peace before that happened.

"Sweet dreams, Jonny."

"Sweet dreams," he would reply.

"Night."

"Night," he'd echo.

"I love you."

"I love you too," he'd say, starting to sound annoyed.

"God bless you."

"God bless you," he'd snort. I could tell he was getting frustrated.

"You too!"

"YOU TOO!" he'd yell back, totally exasperated.

So, to try and avoid the long speech each night, I decided to shorten my goodnight phrases. I'd take the first letter of each word and arrange them to make an acronym: *SNIGY*. *SNIGY* would be the word to help me communicate to my brother how I really felt about him. That would surely help shorten our nighttime routine. Later that night, I explained it to my brother and decided to try out the new phrase.

"SNIGY," I shouted from across the hall.

"SNIGY," he shouted back.

I sat there in silence for a while. But then...my thoughts took over.

What if this is the last night? I can't just end with the word SNIGY. *There's got to be more than that.*

"Sweet dreams, night, I love you, God bless you, you too!! SNIGY!" I yelled back at him.

"SNIGY!!!" came the fed-up, angry shout echoing down the hall. He. Was. Done. Totally done. And the tone of his voice clearly told me that I'd gone too far with this.

My brother and I often tell this story now, giving our friends a glimpse of our childhood, and we laugh at the absurdity of it all. But really, I see the roots. The roots that make up who I am today, stretching back all the way to who I was as a child.

Your Childhood Self

"Tell us one story from your childhood that represents who you are today."

We were having dinner with friends one evening when that conversation starter came up. It was so interesting hearing everyone tell a story from when they were a child that spoke to their personality, quirks, and temperament now as adults. My husband, John, told a story about when he was lifting weights in high school the day before he went off to college. One of the heavy weights on the machine got jammed as he was going up for another bicep curl. He tugged it hard, then harder, then so hard that it flung up right toward his face, slamming into his two front teeth. After recovering from the shock of the blow, he felt something hard moving around the inside of his mouth. He spit it out, and there were two significantly large pieces of his front teeth. He had literally broken a half-moon-shaped portion out of his smile. So, what did he do next, you're wondering? Personally, my high school self would have FREAKED OUT and run out of the gym in a panic to call my mom and frantically ask her to make me an appointment at the nearest dentist she could find! But John? He took the two pieces of his front teeth, put them in his pocket, and casually finished lifting his set. I kid you not. That, my friends, is my husband. He's so laid back and even keeled (sometimes *too laid back*, in my humble opinion!). It takes a lot to get him worked up. He's cool and calm under pressure, and it's so interesting to trace the roots of who he was then to the person he is today.

Who you were then impacts who you are today. What you experienced then influences who you are today. Your childhood personality, experiences, and memories have all come together to shape you into the person you have become. I wonder what story you would tell from your childhood if you were sitting around the dinner table with us. Some stories are benign and laughable, like John's story of lifting weights. Other stories trace the struggles of childhood to the struggles of today, like my underlying anxiety. And other stories are tainted by pain or rejection, insecurity or shame, trauma or tragedy, abuse or abandonment. So much of the way we do life in the present is impacted by the way we experienced life in the past. If we're not aware of our past, not in tune to how it has shaped us, we'll never be able to recognize the patterns. We'll never be able to break free from the past.

> So much of the way we do life in the present is impacted by the way we experienced life in the past.

Backtracking

If you ever book a counseling session with me, you should know that we're going to spend a lot of time talking about the past. In fact, one of the first things I have you do during our time together is to write out a timeline for me of significant events, starting from your earliest memories, and noting the experiences that have shaped you for both good and bad all the way to today. Why don't you join in this process with me? Let's just pretend we're in a counseling session together right now. Go ahead and grab your laptop, a journal, or a piece of paper and a pen, and write out your own timeline. Think through the experiences that have really impacted you or even changed the course of your life from childhood until today. Think of the significant highs and lows in your life that have influenced who you are today.

Maybe, like me, you dealt with some childhood anxieties. Maybe you experienced the pain of watching your parents go through a difficult divorce. What about the day you came to know Jesus; that incredible, life-changing experience at summer church camp; or some bad friendships you endured in high school? It could have been anything from dealing with difficult parents to attending a new church to failing your college entrance exams. It could have been the death of a loved one or even the death of a dream. Maybe it was the sting of a toxic relationship, experiences in your marriage, or dealing with infertility. There are so many things that shape your life, moving you to become the person you are today. Take some time to think through all of those things, and jot them down in the form of a timeline, starting with your earliest significant memories. To make it easier to visualize, I find it helpful to draw a line going up for the positive experiences along the timeline and a line going down for the harmful ones. If you were my client, this is the timeline we'd begin with in our first session together, talking through each significant event, making connections, and extracting the impact and meaning they've had on your life and development. Because whether or not you want to believe it, each portion matters.

Every now and again, I'll get a client who would rather not go there.

"What does the past have to do with what I'm going through today?" they'll question.

"Everything," I'll respond.

The average person doesn't truly understand how significant their past is in shaping their emotional health. But the *majority* of the issues we're facing in the present have their roots in the experiences of our past. When we focus too much on the present without ever looking at the past, we're like gardeners who are pulling the tops of the weeds without getting to the roots. It's only going to give us short-term relief. Those weeds are going to keep coming back until we can get to the bottom of them.

In Philippians 3:13, Paul reminds us of the importance of "forgetting what is behind and straining toward what is ahead." Our problem as human beings is that we can't simply "forget" unless we first acknowledge, understand, and learn from our past. In order for the past to lose its power over us, we have to go back before we can move forward. We have to *deal* with the past in order to be *freed* from the past.

> We have to *deal* with the past in order to be *freed* from the past.

Bryan's Story

Bryan and his wife, Jessica, scheduled an appointment with me because they were having increased marriage conflict. Jessica was frustrated because she felt like Bryan was always working or accomplishing something *outside of* the home but not investing *in* the home. She was starting to feel like a single mom with the amount of time she was investing in the family without Bryan's help. Not only was he absent physically, but when he was home, he wasn't able to be present. There was always something that needed to be done, to be fixed, or to be cleaned. Bryan was frustrated that instead of gratitude for all he did for the family, he was getting flack for all he didn't do. He couldn't understand how Jessica could nag him when he was working so hard.

You might look at this situation from the outside looking in and think that this couple could use a good dose of communication and conflict management. And that was certainly part of the equation. But it wasn't where I began. Trying to deal with the emotional struggles that presented themselves in this couple's marriage without getting to the root of them is like trying to deal with those weeds we talked about earlier without getting to the roots. In order to move forward, we had to backtrack. I spent some time talking one-on-one with Bryan, with his wife listening quietly nearby. We unpacked some of his history to see if we could make sense of the influences from his past that were continuing to shape his present.

Bryan was the oldest of three sons. He was the typical first child in that he was naturally responsible and driven and motivated. But added to that, he grew up with a father who wasn't responsible at all, as Bryan explained it. "My father couldn't be relied on. He never got things done and didn't do what he said he was going to do. It was the running joke in the house if Dad said he was going to fix something; we would all roll our eyes because there was a good chance that it would stay broken forever. He was unmotivated, undisciplined, and always in and out of jobs when I was growing up. He was never there for me emotionally or physically, really. I felt like I couldn't rely on him, so I didn't. I relied on myself."

Later on, in his teen years, tragedy hit when Bryan's father passed away. And his mother was left to care for three boys on her own. Bryan stepped up and filled in the gap even more than he'd done before. He did whatever his mother needed, fixed things around the house, and got a part-time job after school so he could make extra money to help support the family. Through young adulthood, Bryan immersed himself in working hard and took pride in his responsibility. He eventually met and married Jessica—one of the most caring and loving individuals he'd ever laid eyes on. Things were going great, he thought. But fast-forward a few years, and now they were sitting here, meeting with a counselor, on the brink of divorce. He just couldn't make sense of where things had gone wrong.

But what Bryan had failed to realize is that he was living out of the wounds of his past. So accustomed to his emotionally unavailable father and the lack of connection he experienced growing up, Bryan slowly turned that part off in his own life. He failed to learn how to deeply connect with the people around him and instead found his value in what he could do for the people around him. Bryan was still playing a role that he had been playing ever since he was a child. But this time, it was beginning to destroy his relationship with his wife—a woman who was looking for deep and intimate connection from a man who had "turned off" his emotional connection.

My time with Bryan and Jessica was spent unpacking the experiences of his childhood and making connections to how he was living out of those wounds in the present—in his relationship with Jessica. He had to come to terms with the fact that part of the reason why he was so comfortable with a lack of emotional intimacy was because he never truly experienced it! From my experience as a professional counselor, I've seen time and time again how much of our emotional health is shaped by the experiences of our past. Because it's often easier to choose what is familiar rather than what is healthy.

> It's often easier to choose what is familiar rather than what is healthy.

It was only *after* we made those connections that we were able to talk about strategies to overcome the obstacles their marriage was facing. Because once you've identified the root, you begin to have power over it. Little by little, Bryan and Jessica were able to allow God to bring healing to their relationship, but it had to start with going back and getting healing from the past.

Underneath the Surface

We all have experiences, struggles, and wounds that have shaped us into who we are today. So much of our emotional health in the present is built on the experiences of our past—things we may not even be fully aware of at this point in time. Psychologists have long referred to this concept by using the analogy of the iceberg.

When we look at an iceberg, we only see the portion that is above the water. But that's a very small part of the iceberg in its entirety. The majority of the iceberg is actually underneath the surface. Human emotions are the same in that what we see above the surface (that is, how we're acting and feeling in the present) is only a small portion of the big picture of who we are and what we're experiencing. But often the part that's underneath the surface is unknown even to us. Some psychologists refer to that portion as our "unconscious mind," meaning the part we're unaware of. In order to get a full picture of who we are and why we do what we do, we need to take the time to dive deep and go underneath the surface to find out what's really going on inside.

Proverbs 20:5 puts it this way: "The purposes of a person's heart are like deep waters, but one who has insight draws them out." You are not made up of what you see on the surface. In fact, there's so much more to you than you realize. Your heart—your emotions—are like deep waters. But getting to those deep waters requires intention. It requires work. It requires effort. This verse reminds us that having insight is not just something that magically happens. Having insight is an *active* experience; it requires you to "draw out" the deep waters from the well of your life. That would have been such a significant analogy for those living in ancient times. Unlike those of us living in the twenty-first century who just turn on the faucet and enjoy an ice-cold drink, in order to have drinking water, our ancestors had to put in the work. They had to take their buckets and let them down into the well. They had to "draw out" water one bucket at a time, which required energy, persistence, and intention. To say that a person's heart is made up of "deep waters" reminds us that it takes intentional work to get to the bottom of who we are. It takes work that, in my clinical experience, the average Christian has not actually learned how to do.

How Are You, *Really*?

The side of you that people see is only a small part of who you are—when you walk into work, enter church on Sunday mornings and say hello to the people around you, when you walk into the grocery store and chitchat with the cashier on your way out, or as you sit down with a friend for a cup of coffee. This is the side of you that's above the surface—the part that people can see. But it's not the full perspective. If we think about the image of the iceberg, we realize the small portion that others see is only skimming the surface of who you are.

Have you ever run into someone while you were out and about running errands or at a restaurant or at the grocery store or wherever, and they ask that all-too-common question? "So, how are you?" I always find myself struggling with an internal battle whenever I hear that question. Usually, I respond with the typical response of, "I'm good, thanks! How are you?" But internally, I'm thinking: *Well, how much do you really want to know? Let me talk you through the stressors of today. The kids were just out of control. And then earlier this week, I was feeling pretty sick, which led to difficulty sleeping, which led to exhaustion, which retriggered some of my old patterns of anxiety that I know affected my reaction to the kids. It can be so difficult to battle with underlying anxiety and make sure it's kept in check, you know? And honestly, John and I had a little argument this morning before I went out, so I'm dealing with feelings of disappointment and hurt from that. When I get back from the store, we're going to have to talk through some of those emotions. And to top it all off, I'm frustrated that this store was out of my favorite brand of yogurt, which is exactly why I drove an extra ten minutes to come to this side of town. And now, here I am talking to you! Go figure!*

I'm sure that response would go over well, don't you think? It would probably guarantee they'd never ask me how I'm doing ever again. But what's interesting is to see how accustomed we are to just sharing the tip of the iceberg. In fact, it's almost *strange* to share much more than that. We can get so used to living on the tip of the iceberg that we forget there's more going on underneath the surface. We can easily fool ourselves into thinking that what's on the surface is all there is, without ever taking the time to see how we're *really* doing. In just a few minutes of going underneath the surface in my internal conversation that never actually happened, I was able to identify feelings of anxiety, stress, frustration, hurt, disappointment, and exhaustion. That's what's going on underneath the surface. That's how I'm *really* doing. But that's typically what gets suppressed, ignored, or forgotten.

We need to take the time and energy and intention to figure out how we are *really* doing. We need to make it a part of our regular routine and rhythms of our day. That's not to say we need to share that side of us with every Joe and Suzy that we run into at the store (in fact, you're probably better off not sharing), but it does mean we need to actively put in the effort to acknowledge what's really going on under-neath—before the pressure rises, and it comes up on its own.

The Volcano Effect

On an average day in 1815, the earth shook with one of the world's most massive volcanic eruptions. Mount Tambora in Indonesia exploded, sending rivers of molten lava down the mountain and a plume of gases, ash, and rock 12 miles into the atmosphere. The impact of this violent shake triggered dangerous tsunamis all around the island, and over 10,000 people living on the island were instantly killed by the impact of the eruption.[1] Mount Tambora's eruption had a devastating impact on the environment, and scientists can trace its aftermath all the way to environmental consequences in the present. The massive amount of debris from the explosion caused what historians call "the year without a summer":

> Debris from the volcano shrouded and chilled parts of the planet for many months, contributing to crop failure and famine in North America and epidemics in Europe. Cli-mate experts believe that Tambora was partly responsible for the unseasonable chill that afflicted much of the North-ern Hemisphere in 1816.[2]

A volcanic eruption is powerful, impacting both the present as well as the future.

The most interesting thing about a volcanic eruption is what's going on underneath the surface. The scalding heat from the earth's center melts the rock, causing a fiery pool of magma to build up underneath the ground. The thickness of the magma traps pockets of air, and over time, the air bubbles trying to escape cause a powerful amount of pres-sure to build up. Eventually, the buildup of the pressure is so strong that the magma finds the point of least resistance to escape and explodes in the form of a volcanic eruption. It causes devastation to the people around it, as well as ongoing damage to the environment for years to come.

Emotions are much the same way. When we continue to ignore, repress, avoid, or stuff what's going on underneath the surface, we create a natural buildup of pressure. Emotions aren't meant to be stuffed. They're meant to be expressed and shared and dealt with. They're meant to be experienced and used as a compass to guide us and a signal to warn us. But the more we ignore what's actually going on underneath and avoid dealing with the things we're feeling, the more we allow the pressure to build up until, eventually, it finds the point of least resistance and makes its way to the surface. Eventually, we explode.

There are so many ways your "emotional explosion" can happen. For me, it was the unexpected surge of anxiety that led to a paralyzing panic attack on a safari bus. For Bryan, whom I mentioned earlier in the chapter, it was the inability to connect with his wife and children that wreaked havoc on his relationships. For others, it takes the form of explosive anger or rage. For still others, it comes in the form of depression, shutting down, and withdrawing from the world around them. Sometimes, it can take on the form of a physical illness like insomnia, digestive issues, migraines, or palpitations, or a host of other things. Other times, it can come as a mental block—an inability to concentrate, focus, and think clearly. But either way, emotions are a powerful force. When left unchecked, they can impact everything and take away from our ability to live life to the fullest.

Getting in Tune with Our Emotions

Out of all the phrases I hear as a counselor, there's one that I hear come out of people's mouth more than any other phrase: "I don't know." My job as a counselor is to ask a lot of reflective and probing questions. Questions to get people to think, open up, and respond. Questions to spark conversation and get people to dig a little deeper to find the answers. But more often than not, upon my asking a question for the first time, the immediate response I get from people is, "I don't know."

The most interesting part about this phrase is that it comes so instantly, so naturally—almost like an automatic response. They've barely heard my question, much less had time to think about it when I hear the response of "I don't know." Sometimes I wonder if we're wired to respond so quickly because we're not used to the discipline of silence and contemplation. We're not used to taking the time to sit with a question before we answer. Or maybe we're simply uncomfortable with quiet. We feel the pressure to respond right away, and even if the response is, "I don't know," we assume that's better than saying nothing.

> We're not used to the discipline of silence and contemplation.

Before we go on, I want you to do away with that notion that you have to have an instant answer. I want you to get comfortable with sitting with a question for a little while. I want you to take the time to contemplate and formulate a response before you automatically assume you don't know. Because in a few moments, I'm going to ask you some questions. Questions to help us get underneath the surface and take inventory of how you might be feeling deep down. What emotions you might have building up pressure, with or without your awareness. In order to deal with the pressure of emotions, we have to first learn to identify them.

Dr. Robert Plutchik is the psychologist credited for identifying eight basic human emotions: joy, trust, fear, surprise, sadness, anticipation, anger, and disgust.[3] He's credited for using a color wheel, pairing emotions with different colors, as well as shades of color based on the intensity of that particular emotion. For instance, if the emotion of joy is represented by the color yellow, then serenity—a less intense version of joy—would be represented as a light yellow, while ecstasy—a more intense version of joy—would be portrayed in a dark yellow.

I love the color-wheel analogy because it really helps to organize emotions and see them on a scale of intensity, which is an important thing to be aware of. It also helps us to see that there are "opposite"

emotions, such as joy and sadness. Plutchik even goes so far as to identify in-between emotions, which are a "mixture" of two primary emotions that lead to another emotion. For example, the emotion of joy
plus the emotion of trust equal the emotion of love. Just like colors can
be mixed to produce new colors, emotions can be combined to create
new emotions.

Whenever I'm counseling children, one of the first things I do in
our sessions is take a piece of paper and draw an outline of a body. Usually it looks sort of like a gingerbread man, but my bad artwork is just
one of my tactics to break the ice. Or so I tell myself. I then have the
children identify what emotions they "feel in their body" by coloring
in the amount of that emotion that correlates with a specific color. You
can learn a lot about a person based on the feelings they color in their
body. And what's interesting about this activity is you really have no
way of predicting what they'll color. For example, I often do this activity with my own children as a way to check in with them emotionally.
One specific season, my son was having a lot of angry moments, so I
sat him down to color in the feelings in his body. I predicted I'd see a lot
of "red" in his body, representing the anger he was feeling inside. But
at the end of the assignment, his body was mostly filled with yellow—
joy. He had a little bit of red—anger—but he was able to identify what
was making him angry, deal with it, and then move on.

My daughter, on the other hand, is usually the child that presents
as "happy" on the outside. But when we sat down to work on the feelings in her body, her person was filled with a lot of fear and worry. She
deals with anxiety (some hereditary, thanks to her momma), and her
sensitivity keeps her keenly aware of the things she's worried about. But
from the outside looking in, you wouldn't be aware of it.

This is why it's important for us to learn to go underneath the surface. Being in tune with your emotions isn't something you're born
knowing how to do. It's something you have to practice. Kids don't naturally know how to identify and express their emotions. They have to
be taught to do it, sort of like the way I'm teaching my kids. If they're

not taught, they grow up to be adults who don't know how to identify and express their emotions. Because time alone doesn't make us emotionally aware people. The only thing that can move us into emotional awareness is intentionality. We've got to be intentional about going under the surface and finding out what's really going on.

Colors in Our Body

I believe that our inability to deal with our emotions is often rooted in a lack of awareness of our emotions. If we can't identify them, we can't express them. If we can't express them, we can't deal with them. Research has shown that when we become aware of our emotions and start talking about them, our awareness begins to produce positive emotional change in our body. One specific study measured the emotional response of people who were angry. When the subjects were asked about their emotions and responded by processing their emotions, their anger response showed a significant decrease.[4] Awareness matters because it requires us to dig deep and find out what's really going on underneath the surface. It shifts the power from our emotions to ourselves. They are no longer in control—we are.

> Awareness shifts the power from our emotions to ourselves.

It's important to make emotional awareness a regular part of your life. What emotional colors are in your body right now? And how are those emotions impacting your life and well-being? Let's take a deeper look at a few common emotions:

Joy is generally described as a feeling of happiness. Physiologically speaking, it's a flood of dopamine and serotonin to the brain that induces a feeling of euphoria. For some people, joy is a common emotion. They get out of bed in the morning feeling that wonderful sense that all is well in the world. For others, joy might seem hidden, hard to reach, crowded out by other emotions. How would you assess the level of joy you have in your life right now? What are the things that bring you joy in this season of life? When is the last time you woke up feeling that sense of joy? Is there anything that could be preventing you from feeling a sense of joy?

Trust is a feeling of confidence and security. It's a feeling of safety with someone or something. There are things that can influence our feelings of trust—namely, our past experiences and our present experiences. Sometimes the reason we have a hard time feeling trust toward someone is because they have not proven to be a safe person. But other times, the feeling of trust is inhibited because of things we've experienced in the past that keep us from trusting people in the present— even when they've proven themselves to be safe and secure. Trust is an important emotion because it facilitates and strengthens our relationships. It helps us to keep safe people in and unsafe people out. How would you assess the level of trust you have in your life right now? What is adding to your ability to trust, and what is taking away from your ability to trust? Can you differentiate safe people you can trust from unsafe people you can't trust?

Fear is an important emotion because it alerts us to the presence of danger. It sends signals to our brain to tell us to get ready and be prepared. Physiologically, we can find ourselves sweating, our hearts racing, and our minds sharp and alert during times of fear. People experience fear for many different reasons—from a fear of heights, to a fear of germs, to a fear of public speaking. And oftentimes, we can feel the feelings of fear even when there's no present danger (we'll talk a little more about this in coming chapters). How much fear do you have in your body right now? What type of things illicit a feeling of fear? What are you afraid of right now? Do you ever find yourself wondering if there's too much fear in your life?

Sadness alerts our body of the need to be comforted. Dr. Paul Ekman identifies sadness as the feeling we have in the wake of a loss— "a loss of someone or something important."[5] But what defines a loss is different to different people. It could be the loss of a friend, family member, or spouse. The loss of trust, love, or peace. The loss of control or security. Maybe even the loss of a possession such as money, time, power, or popularity. What is the level of sadness you are feeling in this season of life? What are the things that elicit a sense of sadness? Have you experienced any losses that are having an impact on you? What might be going on underneath the surface?

Anger tends to be identified as the emotion we experience when we don't get what we want, or when we get what we don't want. It can happen as a result of injustice, betrayal, rejection, abandonment, or any form of mistreatment. Anger is our instinctive stance to "fight" and can commonly turn into physical aggression as well. It's often been said that anger is a secondary emotion because underneath anger is usually another feeling that has yet to be identified and expressed. I like that theory because I have seen that to be true in my personal life as well as in the lives of clients. When I'm angry, there's usually another emotion fueling that—such as hurt, frustration, disappointment, fear, embarrassment, or pain. When I'm working with clients who are angry, I tend to view "anger management techniques" almost like a Band-Aid. They can't actually help unless we peel back the layers of anger to find out the emotions that are causing it. Are you dealing with any anger in your life right now? If you had to use another word to describe what's going on underneath the anger, what word would you use? What type of things tend to make you angry, and why do you think that is? In what ways is anger impacting your life and your relationships?

> When I'm angry, there's usually another emotion fueling that—such as hurt, frustration, disappointment, fear, embarrassment, or pain.

Disgust is a feeling of aversion toward something or even someone. We can be disgusted by something if it impacts our senses in a negative way (i.e., if it smells or tastes bad), but we can also be disgusted by someone if we interpret their actions or behaviors as offensive. Are there any situations that have caused you to feel a general sense of disgust?

Is there anyone you find yourself avoiding or averting because you're offended by how they act or behave? Is there anything in yourself that gives you the feeling of disgust, and why could that be? How is this feeling impacting your life overall?

Pressure Check

Now that we've gone through some of the basic emotions, I want to ask you a question, and I want you to take your time to answer: Are you *really* okay? How are you really doing? What's going on underneath the surface that might be building up pressure and impacting you from the inside out? There are so many triggers (things that bring about an emotional response) that go unnoticed and unidentified in our day-to-day lives. But something you need to know about triggers is that the more you ignore them, the more pressure begins to build. Our emotional eruption isn't about the trigger itself but about the thousands of emotions that have been building and pent up over time—unexpressed and unaddressed.

There's an inventory that counselors and psychologists often use to get an idea of how many triggers or stressors are building up underneath the surface and potentially causing the buildup of pressure and emotions. It's called the Holmes-Rahe Life Stress Inventory.[6] It breaks down different emotional stressors on a scale of most stressful to least stressful. What's interesting to note about this scale—and something many people don't take into consideration—is that positive life experiences can also cause stress, not just negative ones. Let me give you an example. According to the Holmes-Rahe Life Stress Inventory, getting divorced is one of the top ten stressors on the list, but so is getting married! Both experiences, as different as they are, require change and adjustment. Anytime you go through major changes, there's an element of stress and emotional pressure you need to be aware of.

In his book *Walking on Water When You Feel Like You're Drowning*, world-renowned pastor Tommy Nelson, one of my favorite Bible teachers, very vulnerably talked about his journey through an emotional breakdown at one of the highest moments of his career. He was teaching, preaching, and sharing the gospel on so many platforms, feeling like he was in the prime of his ministry life, when all of a sudden, one day the "explosion" happened. The stress of the pace of his life and the pressure of his emotions underneath the surface finally got to him. He was struck with his very first panic attack a few moments before he got on stage to preach. One thing that struck me most about his story is that there wasn't anything "bad" going on in his life. In fact, it was mostly good things. Good things that required a lot of time, concentration, commitment, and emotional energy. Good things that he enjoyed doing, yet were causing an underlying pressure.[7] Whether from the roots of your past or from the pressure in your present, taking the time to go underneath the surface and get to the bottom of how you really are is an important discipline that you need to build into your life.

I want you to take a moment to go through the Holmes-Rahe Stress Inventory that you'll find at my website, TrueLoveDates.com/resources/, and mark off as many of the life stressors that you've experienced in the last 12 months. After you've done so, add them up to get a final score.

Now, I want you to look at your score as a reminder that both good things and hard things in life can cause pressure. The important thing is that you learn to identify what's going on underneath the surface and learn to release the pressure by acknowledging the experience, being aware of the emotions, talking through it, and finding support. Like I mentioned above, simply being aware of our emotions can decrease their negative impact on our lives. It's important to be in tune with what's going on underneath the surface so you can be active in decreasing the pressure to the best of your ability. We'll talk about additional methods to decrease that pressure later on in the book.

Taking Inventory

Becoming aware and going underneath the surface is the first step toward emotional health. As you get ready to go deeper into the journey of emotional health, I challenge you to start taking notes. Being intentional about getting healthy means you can't just read about it—you have to actually go after it. Grab an empty journal that you will use to write and reflect on the "checkup" exercises at the end of each chapter of this book. Write out the questions, and then think through the answer before you begin to write. I suggest you also note the date at the top of each page to keep track of your journey and make it easier to look back at your progress and change. Allow this to be an interactive experience for you, where you're not just reading the information but applying it as well. The more you put into this, the more you'll get out of it.

Journaling Questions: 5-Minute Emotional Checkup

- What are the triggers, problems, struggles, stressors, adjustments, or changes that I find myself dealing with today?

- On a "Pressure Scale" of 1 to 10 (10 being the most pressure), how much pressure do I feel like I'm dealing with underneath the surface?

- Are the emotions I present to the world (the top of the iceberg) similar to what I am feeling inside (underneath the surface)? If not, what might really be going on underneath the surface?

- List the most common emotions you have experienced in the past 12 months, as well as what causes those emotions. Which one of those emotions do you tend to experience most often? In what type of situations do these emotions tend to come up?

- Do I have "safe people" to express what's going on underneath the surface?
    - o If so, who? How can I begin letting them into what's going on underneath?

o If not, what are some steps I can take to invite people
   into my life?

- What are some ways I can begin the process of investing in
  my emotional awareness?

2

Patterns Lead to Process

Emotional History

I've had an on-again, off-again relationship with anxiety and depression. For the most part, those uncomfortable emotions are like a hot spring—always there, but quietly bubbling under the surface of the ground. Most of the time, they stay below the surface, under control, manageable, and unable to be seen by others around me. In fact, I've even gotten to a point where I often forget they're there. I've gone through seasons where they've remained quiet for so long, I almost believed they didn't exist anymore. But every now and again when life gets too crazy or the kids get too overwhelming or my hormones get too wacky, the pressure will bring those emotions up to the surface again. They burst into my life like uninvited guests.

I remember the very first time these uninvited guests barged into my life. I was a graduate student, studying to get my master's in counseling.

Why is that an important fact? Because it reiterates the idea that no one is immune to the intruder of uncomfortable emotions—not even counseling students, professional counselors, doctors, lawyers, teachers, preachers, or little eight-year-old kids who say "SNIGY" before bed.

I remember waking up during that stage of life, feeling a wave of despair come over me, but for absolutely no reason that I could logically formulate. Which made it even more difficult to deal with. It's one thing when you have a clear reason why you're feeling down, but it's a whole other story when you know that life is good—even great—yet you can't seem to shake the feelings of discouragement and despair. Now, looking back, there were actually many different factors that likely led to that point in my life—and I'll get to those a little later on—but I definitely didn't recognize them then. I don't think I even had enough energy to try to make sense of it.

I would wake up feeling awful. Especially on Monday mornings. Why Mondays, you ask? I really don't know. Maybe it was the start of a new week, and the pressure that week held was unconsciously pressing down on me. Maybe it was because Mondays were the only day of the week that I woke up with nowhere to be, which meant less of a distraction from how I was feeling. Or maybe because Mondays were the morning after the weekend, it meant the time to rest was over, and now it was time to push myself back into a routine of work and study. I'm not really sure. But Mondays were especially awful.

I remember many Monday mornings, rolling out of bed and desperately picking up my phone within moments of opening my eyes. The weight of the awful feelings flooded me like an ocean wave violently being hurled at my chest. I would call my mom, who lived hours away, and burst into tears at the sound of her calming voice.

"I don't know why I feel so terrible," I would lament to her.

"It's okay, habibi" (which affectionately means "my love" in her native Arabic), she would calmly reply, with a choked-up voice. And listen. And cry with me. I don't remember how long that specific season lasted—probably close to six months. Six difficult, dark months.

Fast-forward about four years. The uninvited guests of depression and anxiety came back into my world once again, just a few weeks after what was supposed to be one of the happiest moments of my life. Talk about an unexpected turn of events. I was now a few years into marriage, and I had delivered our first baby after a long and traumatic birth experience. Ella was positioned in my uterus in such an unexplainable way that she got stuck in the birth canal on her way into the world. I'll spare you the details, but anyone who has ever birthed a baby (or watched it happen) knows how tiresome it can be. After 17 hours of labor, I had to actively push for an additional three and a half hours. It felt impossible. Imagine running an entire marathon, getting to the end feeling like you're about to pass out and throw up, and then being told, "Just kidding, this isn't the end. In fact, you have to turn around and run it again." I just couldn't do it. I remember telling the doctor I'd be okay with leaving the baby in there for another few years until I recovered. Somehow, I managed to crack a joke even as I felt like I was dying. But since no one agreed to let me leave her in there, I had to keep going, enduring what would become the most physically straining three and a half hours of my life.

It was all worth it in the end because Ella was born, and I was instantly filled with joy. But the joy was short-lived because, moments later, the joy turned into panic. When they placed her in my arms, she was blue and quiet—not pink and crying like most babies. The severe shock from being in the birth canal for so long had not only traumatized but also injured her. I barely got one look at her, and within moments she was rushed to the NICU.

Ella spent the next few days in the care of incredible doctors and nurses in the NICU, recovering from two collapsed lungs and bleeding in her skull. John and I stayed in the hospital for those four days, praying and dreaming of bringing our baby home. Praise the Lord, she fully recovered, and we brought her home to begin adjusting to our new normal—an adjustment no parent is ever fully prepared for.

I remember exactly when I started feeling like things weren't okay.

It was the five-week mark of bringing Ella home. Five weeks of lacking sleep, five weeks of trying to get her to nurse to no avail, five weeks of dealing with a fussy baby with no end in sight. I think I held on to hope because someone told me that the five-week mark after delivering a baby was a point of respite. But it arrived, and I was only feeling worse with each passing day. And all of a sudden, the wave of despair came over me once again. The uninvited guests of anxiety and depression barged into my world with no reserve.

I struggled to sleep at night, and when I finally dozed off, I would wake up in the middle of the night in a panic, feeling like my body was on fire and drenched in sweat. My mind would race, and I couldn't get it to stop. I lost my appetite and could barely look at food without feeling nauseous (and with how much I *love* food, you know something is seriously wrong when my appetite is gone). And worst of all, I lost my joy. My days were flooded with feeling anxious and overwhelmed. I found my mind always wandering to worst-case scenarios and fears— fears about my baby, her well-being, her health. Fears that I wasn't being a good enough mom. The fears turned into shame—shame that I couldn't nurse her the way I wanted to. Shame that I wasn't feeling joy during what's supposed to be the happiest moments of my life. The shame welled up inside of me and burst out into a flood of tears. Oh, the tears I cried during that season of my life! I barely recognized myself. What had happened to me? Where had the "real me" gone? Would I ever go back to the person I used to be?

These uninvited guests came back a few more times over the next few years of my life. They popped in for a few weeks after my second child, Eli, was born. And then about a year after that, when I was facing significant stressors in my life, they came back for another unwanted visit. Two years later, they showed up again after a big family move to Florida. I had hoped I left them in Pennsylvania, but there they were— not as obvious this time, but still there. And then once again five years later, they showed up in the form of an unexpected panic attack...a panic attack on a safari bus. Of all places.

But the thing about these uninvited guests is this: Each time they came, I began to recognize them a little faster. I began to notice when things inside me were starting to shift, to change, to feel different. I started recognizing patterns and had an idea of what to look for. And eventually, I learned what to do to keep them under control when they did come along, and at times, prevent them from coming along altogether. I learned to expect them, to be prepared for them, and to have what I needed to keep them at bay...until they decided to go back to where they came from. The most important part of my healing came when I learned to recognize the patterns and learn from them.

Recognize the Patterns

Patterns are everywhere. We're not typically aware of them, but they're there when we look for them. We're creatures of habit, and we tend to do things the same way without always realizing that we're caught in a pattern.

Each one of us has a pattern to the way we do life. The patterns that we follow eventually become our process—the *why* to what we do and what we feel. Our process shapes and impacts every part of our life. Patterns become process. If we want to change our process, we have to start by recognizing our patterns.

> Patterns become process.

Patterns can be so ingrained in us that it's not always easy to recognize them. Sometimes, it's easier for others to see them before we do. When I was in college, I was made aware of certain dining patterns I had that were unbeknownst to me. During lunch in the cafeteria, my friends would make comments about the way I did certain things. Take, for example, how I make and eat a sandwich. First, I have to start with two slices of even bread. What I mean by that is one slice can't be bigger than the other, and you definitely can't use that end part of the loaf, affectionately known as "the nub" in the Fileta home. That's the "bookend" of the loaf, and that imposter is meant for nothing but to be thrown away.

God's Word tells us not to be unequally yoked, so why not apply that to how we make a sandwich? (Okay, that's taking it a little too far.)

Anyway, once I have my two slices of bread, I evenly distribute the mayonnaise on each side, followed by a long, even, back-and-forth swirl of the mustard. Heavier on the mayo is my style. I'll choose one side to pile the meat and cheese, and the other side for the lettuce and tomato. Then I smash the sandwich together and slice it right down the middle in half. I eat it one half at a time, making sure I always start from the inside of the sandwich out to the crust.

I didn't know there was any other way to eat a sandwich until my friends started noticing my patterns and calling me out on my tactics. My patterns turned into my process—the way I do things—in this case, the way I eat a sandwich. My sandwich-eating habits don't really impact the rest of my life, but what about the patterns that turn into a process in important areas of life? Imagine the things we could be doing without even being aware of them.

Creatures of Habit

You are also a creature of habit. You come to the table with patterns in what you feel, how you think, and what you do. In fact, research shows us that it's not necessarily what you *want* that makes you do the things you do; it's the strength of your habits.[1] The more you do something, the more likely you are to do it again. As one study puts it, "In domains in which patterns can develop, frequent performance in the past reflects habitual patterns that are likely to be repeated automatically in future responses."[2] In other words, your intentions take a backseat to your patterns.

> What ends up winning in the end is what you *practice* regularly.

Even if you *want* to do something differently, what ends up winning in the end is what you *practice* regularly. Patterns have a tendency to trump intentions.

Take, for instance, how you fold your hands together. Take a second to fold your hands. Which thumb is on top? Your right thumb, or left thumb? For me, it's my left thumb that finds its way to the top (even though I'm right-handed). I wish there was some cutting-edge research behind all this, telling you that people who are predominately left-thumb dominant are brighter, smarter, or—better yet—sell more books...but there isn't. It is what it is: a pattern. You'll see what I mean in just a moment because now I want you to put the book down again, and this time, I want you to try your hardest on the count of three, to quickly fold your hands together again but this time trying to let the thumb of the *opposite* hand rest on top. Ready? One...two...three.

How did you do? If you're anything like me, or the majority of people who do this exercise, it took you a second to get it right! You had to really think about it this time. And maybe you couldn't even do it! And if you think *that's* hard, you should try crossing your arms next and seeing which hand tends to rest on top and then trying the opposite. I can barely get that one right even when I'm really concentrating.

Here's the thing about it: Your body has been doing the same thing for so long that it eventually becomes the default way of how you do things. It's automatic. It's second nature. It's a pattern that you practice that eventually turns into a process—*your* process. The same goes for so many other areas in your life. The more you feel, do, think, or experience something, the more it becomes part of your process.

The human brain is malleable, meaning it can be influenced. When your brain—the supercomputer that controls your emotions, thoughts, and body—is exposed to the same or a similar thing over and over again, it naturally begins repeating those things without your permission.

One of the ways I teach this concept to clients is by having them picture water trickling down a mountain. Eventually, the water will come down to the point of least resistance, creating a path. More water will trickle down that same path, and eventually, a groove will form in the rock, allowing for more water to pass through. Before you know it, you have a river that's getting deeper and deeper with each pass through.

Our brains work much the same way. The more we implement patterns into our life, the more set in our ways we become. And this is why it's *crucial* to begin recognizing our patterns. Because patterns lead to our process, and process leads to the way we do life.

From Patterns to Process

When it comes to emotional health, it's extremely important to understand that there is a certain set of patterns that you engage in *as well as* patterns that have been passed down to you. Patterns in what you feel, that influence how you think, which in turn impact what you do. Patterns that have been passed down from your parents, that they learned from their parents, that they learned from their parents. And if you don't recognize those patterns and adjust those patterns as needed, they will eventually become *your* process.

In the book of Exodus, we're introduced to a passage of Scripture that theologians often refer to as the "generational curse," wherein God says to the Israelites, "I, the Lord your God, am a jealous God, punishing the children for the sin of the parents to the third and fourth generation of those who hate me, but showing love to a thousand generations of those who love me and keep my commandments" (20:5-6).

But a generational curse isn't some mystical hocus-pocus. Instead, most theologians agree that it's a pattern that has been passed down from one generation to the next. As Mark Hanegraaff, president of the Christian Research Institute, puts it,

> If your family line is marked by divorce, incest, poverty, anger or other ungodly patterns, you're likely under a generational curse. The Bible says that these curses are tied to choices. Deuteronomy 30:19 says we can either choose life and blessing or death and cursing...Our families have the greatest influence on our development, including the development of our patterns of sin.[3]

Our emotional health is impacted by the generations before us, and it's important for us to recognize the patterns so that we can begin changing the process.

Family Ties

When teaching this concept of family patterns to Christians across the country and world, I often sense a hesitation to identify negative family patterns. As Christians, the importance of honoring our fathers and mothers (Exodus 20:12) has been drilled into our heads to the point where we misinterpret the command to mean we shouldn't have anything negative to say about how we were raised or brought up. In a desire to honor our parents, we can overlook patterns that are harmful or that would shed light on some of the things that we're struggling with today. But honoring our parents doesn't mean we ignore the reality that we are all sinful people who are prone to making mistakes. Our parents, as well-intentioned as many of them often are, are flawed human beings just like the rest of us. Acknowledging the negative patterns we've seen or experienced is meant to help us take personal responsibility and ownership of the quality of the life we're living and the emotions that we're experiencing. Identifying harmful patterns isn't meant to heap blame on those who have gone before us. Instead, it's meant to make it better for those who will come after us. That's how we can break the "generational curse."

> Identifying harmful patterns isn't meant to heap blame on those who have gone before us. Instead, it's meant to make it better for those who will come after us.

It took me well into my young adult years to realize that acknowledging the patterns of my past was not dishonoring my parents. My parents were born and raised in Cairo, Egypt. They immigrated to the United States shortly after they got married. But the patterns that would eventually shape me, their first daughter, came right along with them. My dad grew up as a pastor's son. My grandfather, the pillar of faith in our family, was a traveling evangelist and minister who served God in some of the most anti-Christian cities in Egypt. They had a large family, and living on a pastor's salary during that time meant that they didn't have much to spare. My dad tells me stories of those rare days as a child where he got rewarded with a coin to go spend on a chocolate bar. Growing up, those simple joys were never taken for granted. My grandfather was a hardworking man who dedicated everything he had to the ministry and work of God. And that hard work ethic was naturally passed down to my father. He grew up committed to his studies, and eventually, he moved with my mom to the United States, where he continued his pursuit of becoming a doctor.

Growing up as the daughter of an immigrant, hard work was the theme of my childhood. My parents had to work harder than ever to make it in a country that wasn't their own. Looking back, it's a pattern that was passed down to me from generation to generation. "Don't be lazy," my dad would remind us. "Work hard and do your best." I adopted those patterns as my own and worked hard at everything I did. I was a leader in my church youth group, graduated high school with fantastic grades, worked hard through college taking extra courses—all while holding down a job and actively pursuing ministry. I graduated from college early just so I could start graduate school at the young age of 20 and worked hard to maintain a 4.0 average. But things started to implode for me right around that time when I went through my first episode of depression. My emotional health began catching up to me. I found out the hard way that when taken to the extreme, even good patterns can cause damage.

A lot of what I was feeling about myself during that time had to do with what I was doing or not doing. For so long, I had repeated the patterns of a hard work ethic that when I wasn't *doing* enough (or what I thought wasn't enough), I felt that I was somehow failing. I equated value with doing, rather than with being. Which, ironically, was the exact opposite of the pattern God wanted me to adopt. I was living out of the patterns of my past rather than out of the patterns God had for me.

The Bible tells us that we are fearfully and wonderfully made inside the womb—before we've even had a chance to *do* anything (Psalm 139:14)—and created in the image of God (Genesis 1:27) and chosen by God before the foundations of the world (Ephesians 1:4). There's so much less *do* and so much more *be* throughout the pages of Scripture. It took awhile for me to begin to understand the patterns I had been carrying and allow myself to exchange my patterns for God's. In order for me to find emotional healing, I had to break the cycle of performance-based value and choose to see myself as already wonderful, already chosen, and already loved by God.

Past Patterns

Now that you're starting to get bits and pieces of my story, I wonder if you're starting to think through your own. What are the patterns that have shaped you over time or are still shaping you today? What habits are leading you into healthy interactions or keeping you from them? What are the values or beliefs that have been passed down to you, that are influencing the way that you do life?

> I was living out of the patterns of my past rather than out of the patterns God had for me.

A common tool that we use in counseling to get a picture of our family patterns is called a genogram. A genogram is like an elaborate family tree, but instead of just identifying the date of birth and relationships of each family member, it goes a little deeper into identifying family traits, personalities, characteristics, and relationships.

A genogram focuses on the emotional relationship between people on the family tree, identifying whether the relationship was conflictual, estranged, distant, very close, friendly, or a host of other descriptive words. It tracks marriages and relationship patterns and can even be used to identify dominant positive and negative personality traits of each person on the genogram. It's important to try and include at least three generations as you're thinking through your genogram. Make phone calls, schedule interviews, and initiate conversations with family members who are willing to share. Gather as much information as you can because each person as well as each generation offers more insight into the patterns you've brought into the present.

If you're interested in creating your own genogram, there are loads of resources on the Internet to help get you started, but you can consider creating a basic three-tier genogram in your journal by drawing a family tree that depicts the generation before you (your grandparents on both sides) as well as your parents and their siblings, followed by you and your current family. Some things you can consider making note of in your genogram are the personality traits of each person, their mental health struggles, emotional temperament, and relationship status, as well as the quality of their relationships. Are there any behavioral patterns such as addictions, abuse, divorce, workaholism, relationship conflict, or anything that might resemble a pattern in your family tree? Were there any familial value statements that have been passed down from one generation to the next, dysfunction that seemed to be present in more than one person, or problems and struggles that pop up in more than one generation? This is an important time to take inventory and look for patterns that may have shaped your family tree or have even been passed down to you. As you contemplate your family genogram, consider connecting with a licensed therapist to help you in the process of building and talking through your genogram as you identify emotional patterns and how they might be impacting your life.

Present Patterns

I mentioned earlier that it was only when I started recognizing my patterns that I could begin to learn and heal. There were two parts to the process of recognizing my patterns.

My past patterns: I had to understand the family patterns of my *past* that shaped me into the person I am today (i.e., performance-based worth).

My present patterns: Next, I had to recognize that my *present* patterns were creating a cycle of unwanted emotional experiences. It was just as crucial for me to understand what I was doing in the present that was contributing to the distress in my life and fueling the cycle of depression and anxiety. With regard to present patterns, I want to take some time to talk you through a few common ones that many people tend to struggle with. Maybe you can identify some of these in your personal life as well:

Doing Too Much

Because of my past family patterns, my tendency to want to "do more to be more" is a part of my life I've learned to recognize and be cautious with. It's a wonderful thing to have a drive to work, to engage in ministry, and to be productive. But if I'm not careful, I can find myself doing more than I am able to do and feeling overwhelmed.

Back in graduate school, when depression hit me for the first time, I was studying and going to graduate school all while working part-time at the local psychiatric hospital, as well as leading an entire inner-city ministry. Later on, when depression hit again, I was adjusting to the life of being a new mom, which in and of itself is filled with "doing too much." A year after that, when my second son was born, not only was I juggling the life of a mom of two kids under two, but I was writing my first book and getting my brand-new ministry up and running at TrueLoveDates.com. Needless to say, that's a whole lot to have going on. In each stage when depression hit, there was a pattern of having too much on my plate and doing too much with not enough boundaries intact. But that wasn't the only component...

Hormonal Changes

One of the most significant patterns that I've come to understand is how much hormonal changes impact emotional health. Normally, having too much on my plate would probably just elevate my stress levels. But having too much on my plate *paired* with my hormonal changes is what sets me into a cycle of anxiety and depression.

In graduate school, I had just started taking the birth control pill to try to balance my hormones. That hormonal shift, paired with doing too much, set me into the pit of anxiety and depression. Later on, when my daughter was born, the doing too much of motherhood, paired with the hormonal changes of a postpartum body, was exactly the right recipe to send me into another episode of anxiety and depression. The same with the birth of my second child. And most recently, another hormonal change (restarting the birth control pill after the birth of my third child), on top of having a lot on my plate at the time, was the pattern that triggered the onset of a panic attack on a safari bus. There are so many factors that can play into the patterns that set us into a cycle of emotional struggle, and for me, hormonal changes are something that can't be overlooked in the big picture of identifying emotional triggers.

In counseling, one word we use to describe the patterns that lead to emotional struggle is *triggers*. Two triggers for me are doing too much as well as hormonal changes, but let me list a few more patterns or "triggers" that might be influencing *your* emotional health.

Past Trauma

Our body has an uncanny ability to remember past emotional struggles and respond similarly to events in the present. It's important to recognize patterns because your current emotional distress might have something to do with a past traumatic experience. As I observed my patterns, I was eventually able to make a connection that a certain trauma I had experienced was having a significant impact on my emotional patterns in the present. This is an all-too-common trigger that often goes unnoticed.

One young woman I counseled many, many years ago was struggling with severe episodes of fear and anxiety when she moved into her new apartment with some friends. She would catch herself feeling such intense fear that she would literally freeze going up the stairs, as though her legs were too scared to keep moving. She couldn't understand why her body was responding to this new living situation with such uncontrollable outbursts of fear. She loved her roommates, and she was excited for this new season of independence.

It took some time to unpack this trigger, but by the end of our counseling sessions, it was made clear that the anxiety and fear she was feeling was actually rooted in her past trauma—trauma she had long pushed back and tried to forget. As a small child, she had experienced sexual abuse at the hands of her biological father, and without her conscious awareness, certain features of this new apartment (the flooring, the ceiling, the wall colors) were reminding her body and brain of the place in which the abuse had taken place long ago. *This place is dangerous* is the message it was signaling in her brain, which led to feelings of immense fear and anxiety. Her current distress was rooted in past trauma that she hadn't yet pieced together. But the body doesn't forget, even when the mind tries to, which is why past trauma is such an important piece to understanding our present patterns. We'll spend an entire chapter talking through trauma a little later in the book, but I just want to get us thinking about the vast scope of circumstances or triggers that can impact our emotional response.

Current Life Stress

From job stress to relationship stress, from the stress of raising a family to the stress of managing ministry. Stress increases our cortisol levels (a hormone inside our body), inducing an anxiety response in our body that impacts our emotions as well as our physical health. We can even find ourselves stressed out and struggling because of too many *good* things. This is why we find such a high rate of burnout among pastors and ministry leaders. Just because you're involved in something "good" or ministry focused doesn't mean you'll be immune to the stress that comes with those good things.

Pastor Zach Tims is one example of a person who found himself seriously struggling in the face of a wave of significant life stressors. His story made national headlines when he died of a drug overdose after a series of devastating behaviors, including cheating on his wife. An article written about his tragic situation observed the pattern that often people with a high amount of stress end up doing really "unexpected" things. As Shaun King bluntly puts it,

> Pastor Tims was under a huge amount of pastoral stress, he had major issues from his past that were not resolved, and he had crazy sins that nearly took him under. Instead of removing the pastoral stress, it appears to me that Pastor Tims started working 2-3 times as hard as he was before he had an affair. He preached more, traveled more, was on TV more, etc. In essence, Zach increased his pastoral stress, created less time to deal with unresolved issues, and now he is dead.[4]

Life stress alone doesn't cause emotional breakdown, but when left unchecked and then paired with other triggers, it certainly has the power to break you down. That's why it's important to take inventory of our life stress and make sure we're setting boundaries—acknowledging that we can't do it all, and not only that, but that we shouldn't do it all. It's important to regularly take inventory of how much stress is in our life and then do what we can to decrease it.

Physical Exhaustion

Looking back at the hardest seasons of my life emotionally, sleep was always part of the equation. Sometimes, the very first sign that something is not as it should be is when I find that I'm not sleeping as well as I normally do. Maybe you find that it's taking you a very long time to get settled into sleep at the end of the day because your mind is filled with the buzzing of thoughts. Maybe you find yourself waking up multiple times in the middle of the night—it could be you have a newborn that's keeping you up, or that you just can't seem to stay asleep for one reason or the other. Or maybe you find yourself waking up much earlier than you want to, unable to fall back into a deep sleep. Either way, a lack of sleep or disruption of sleep can severely impact a person's emotional well-being and can be an early signal that something is going on underneath the surface.

If you find yourself struggling more than usual emotionally, it's important to recognize if a lack of sleep hygiene could be a potential trigger. So often, sleep and emotional struggles go hand in hand, and dealing with one often brings stability to the other. If you find yourself struggling with the trigger of sleep deprivation right now, there are natural supplements you can try for better sleep and sleep hygiene methods to follow, as well as medications that we'll discuss further in the physical health section of this book. But for now, keep this topic in your mind as you're taking inventory of the possible triggers that are impacting your emotional health.

Medication Changes

Medication changes can be a trigger for patterns of emotional struggles. Whether you're starting a brand-new medication for the first time or switching over to another one, it's important to be aware that the medication in and of itself can potentially cause emotional side effects. That's not to say that medication should be avoided! I am so grateful for the miracle of modern medicine. But awareness is important so you can identify what might be causing a season of emotional distress and deal with it properly.

I mentioned my prior experience with certain birth control pills, but contraceptives aren't the only medication with potential emotional side effects. And men can be vulnerable to experiencing emotional side effects as much as women. A recent study estimated that over 37 percent of people in America were taking medication where "depression" or "suicidal thoughts" were listed as an adverse side effect.[5] The study went on to explain that the more medications that a person was on which listed a side effect of depression or suicidality, the higher the likelihood that they would experience those specific symptoms. Some of the medications that are known to have emotional side effects include (but are not limited to) acid reflux medication, birth control pills, allergy medication, anxiety medication, blood pressure medication, pain medication, as well as antiseizure medication.[6] It's important to understand the potential trigger of medication on emotional health so that you can make an informed decision and deal with the side effects accordingly. Be sure to discuss any emotional side effects with your doctor, and see if there could be any alternative options for your medications.

Conflict

One of the most common yet unidentified triggers for emotional struggle is experiencing conflict. Dealing with relationship problems can be one of the primary things that impact how you are feeling emotionally. I worked with a young woman who was struggling with a pattern of depression in her life. It seemed to come out of nowhere, and the lack of understanding of her triggers left her feeling completely out of control, paranoid that the feelings could come back at any moment. As we talked through her family history and worked through the timeline of her life, it became clear to me very quickly that in seasons of conflict she tended to fall into a state of depression.

One of the reasons she didn't recognize this pattern is because the conflict looked so different in each situation. Sometimes it was conflict with a boyfriend, other times it was conflict that arose from a struggle with her closest friends, and other times still it was stress and conflict coming from her family. Each set of interactions looked so different that it was hard for her to recognize the one theme that tied them all together: conflict. She was by nature a conflict avoider. The very experience of conflict caused her to feel inadequate, unlovable, and unworthy, which had a direct impact on her emotional well-being.

A huge part of the counseling process for her meant getting to the root of her beliefs about conflict, as well as her beliefs about herself. It meant recognizing conflict as an emotional trigger and finding healthy ways to navigate through conflict. But if she wasn't made aware of this trigger, she would have never been able to deal with it. Emotional health and well-being are often influenced by our closest relationships. It's important to remember that and ask yourself how your closest relationships and interactions have influenced you.

Negative Thinking

So much of how we feel stems from what we think because thoughts lead to feelings. A long time ago, scientists used to think that feelings led to thoughts, and when we felt poorly, we'd begin to think poorly. But the latest psychology points to the reality that it's actually the other way around: Negative thoughts lead to negative feelings, which ultimately lead to negative behaviors. We'll spend some significant time discussing this important topic in the mental health section of the book, but for now it's necessary to understand that your thoughts are an important component of what is triggering your emotional distress.

Health Issues

Because human beings are holistic, there's a strong connection between our bodies, minds, and emotions. When one part of us is unhealthy, the others will certainly struggle. Many times, emotional distress *causes* physical illness. It's common knowledge that too much stress has a detrimental impact on our physical health—from our digestive system, to our energy levels, all the way to our autoimmune response. But the opposite can also happen. Physical health issues can have a domino effect on how we're feeling emotionally.

I counseled a young woman whose chronic physical illness was starting to take a toll on her emotional well-being. Our emotional health and physical health are so intertwined that it can be hard to know which is causing what. Are the physical symptoms causing emotional distress? Or could the emotional distress be leading to physical symptoms? Often, it's a little bit of both, but in this situation, the young woman was dealing with a clearly diagnosed physical illness, but with no prior history of emotional distress. She'd always been a positive person, full of joy, motivation, and energy. But as her physical diagnosis began to take away her energy, she also began to lose her motivation and joy. For her, a huge portion of her counseling plan was focused on managing her physical symptoms as the first step to dealing with her emotional struggles. She had to focus on finding the proper medications, getting the rest she needed, and following a nutritious meal plan so that she could get her body as healthy as possible in order to bring her emotional health back into balance. The important body-mind connection needed to be brought to light, and we'll dive deeper into this concept in the section about physical health.

Financial Concerns

For many people, financial struggles—including dealing with major debt or an inability to save money—is one of the major triggers of emotional distress. Financial issues can come with feeling a lack of control, overwhelm, fear, and shame.

I counseled a young man who would fall into the pit of emotional distress as soon as he felt like he couldn't support his family. He owned a small business, and at times, the financial stream was inconsistent and unreliable. Not being able to provide for his family was one of his primary triggers, and becoming aware of his emotional response to financial concerns was a huge part to gaining control. Eventually, he was able to find freedom from the lies that his value and worth depended on his ability to provide for his family.

It's important to recognize the trigger of financial concerns and enlist the help of a counselor or financial advisor in order to begin taking control of this area of your life.

Change or Loss

Change and loss are common experiences that can trigger emotional distress. I put them in the same category because loss always brings change, and change always brings loss. The two go hand in hand. Whether it's a change of a job or career, location, relationship status, or the loss of a loved one, a reputation, or a marriage, change and loss can leave a void in our life that shakes up our world and leaves us feeling disoriented. They cause us to reconfigure our lives, which often brings about an emotional response.

When I met Marilyn, she was dealing with a tremendous amount of change and loss. She scheduled counseling sessions with me because she was feeling overwhelmed and emotionally distressed. Marilyn's husband had been diagnosed with an aggressive cancer and was bedridden for his last few months of life. She was now left to care for her dying husband, as well as her two young children. Not only that, but she had recently experienced a change in location as, just months before her husband's diagnosis, they had moved their family to a new town. And now she was also experiencing a change of roles, as she moved from being a stay-at-home mom to a working mom in order to meet the financial demands of her household. The tremendous amount of change and loss she was experiencing would cause any human being to feel overwhelmed and distressed.

Marilyn walked through that season of her life with Jesus by her side and her strong faith intact. She eventually experienced the loss of her husband and had to rebuild her life once again after the devastation of loss. Meeting with her weekly and witnessing her walk through this hard season of her life was a constant reminder to me of the God-given strength of the human spirit to overcome hardships in times of immense loss. I often wonder if I impacted her as much as she impacted me.

Your loss might be as great as Marilyn's, or it might seem small in comparison. But loss doesn't have to be tremendous for it to be impactful. Any shift in the balance of your life, any change, opens the door for an emotional response. Not only that, but the more changes you have in a short period of time, the more likely you'll feel the emotional impact. If you're not aware, you won't be able to make the connection. And if you can't recognize the pattern, you'll forfeit the opportunity to change the process.

Taking Inventory

In this chapter, we've talked through the importance of patterns—past and present. What patterns have you experienced in your past that might be having an impact on your present? What personal patterns are you experiencing in the present that are impacting your emotional response or even causing emotional distress? Understanding your emotional history—shedding light on the patterns that you've come from and the patterns that you're repeating—is a crucial step along the journey of emotional health.

So grab your journal, and let's take a few minutes for an emotional checkup.

Journaling Questions: 5-Minute Emotional Checkup

- What patterns have I noticed from my genogram that have been "passed down" to me?

- Do I see any connections between the problems of my present to the experiences of my past?

- What are some experiences from my past that have shaped me in a positive way? What are some experiences from my past that have shaped me in a negative way?

- Out of the list of emotional triggers mentioned, which contribute to my emotional distress and why?

- Consider taking some additional time and using this portion of your journal to draw a genogram. For more details and instructions on this process, check out www.genopro. com/genogram.

3

God Is More Real than My Reality

Emotional Control

Have you ever just had a *feeling* that something was wrong?

It was a damp, dark, foggy fall night, and I was a graduate student at the time living off campus with some of my friends. My roommates and I had just arrived home from church and pulled into the driveway, and right away we noticed that things were not as we had left them. We always make a point of turning off the lights before going out, but as we pulled up to the house, we noticed every single light in the house was on. Right away, our emotions kicked into high alert. *Stay in the car!* one of us said to the others. *Nobody get out!* We sat in eerie silence in the driveway for a few more moments, trying to assess the situation and figure out what we should do. Minus the lights all being on, nothing seemed terribly amiss. I mean, for all we knew, one of us could have left them on without realizing it. It was probably nothing.

Just as soon as we were starting to relax and consider going in the house, all of a sudden, the lights in the house started turning off...one by one. To our horror, we saw a shadow shuffling around inside, and then there was a loud noise that sounded like the intruder might have even tripped on something. Now, we were in *full* panic mode! *Lock the doors! Call 911!* I was in the driver's seat of the parked car, so I locked the car doors and put the car in reverse as fast as I could as one of my room-mates dialed 911. We needed to get out of there and *fast* before who-ever was in there came out! Within seconds, we heard footsteps coming toward us, crunching the small gravel stones of the pavement beneath their feet, getting louder and louder and faster and faster as the intruder got nearer. By this point, everyone in the car was screaming all while we were trying to communicate to the 911 operator that someone had bro-ken into our home. I had already begun backing out of the driveway and was about to make a fast and furious getaway when the driveway floodlights turned on and we saw...our 90-year-old landlord, Mary.

Maaaaaaaaaaarryyyy!!!!!!!!!!!!!!!!! we all shouted. *What on earth were you doing in our house?*

"Well," she said rather nonchalantly, "I'm sorry if I scared you girls, but I really needed a frying pan and couldn't find one in my apartment, so I thought I'd come down here and see if there was one in the storage closet I could find. No one was home, and I have a spare key, so I just let myself in. Hope that's okay."

Oh, Mary.

We were terrified. And even after we found out it was only Mary, it took us awhile to calm down and settle in for the night. We were all a little jumpy for the rest of the evening. Emotions can be powerful. But that begs to ask the question: Can they always be trusted?

Can Emotions Be Trusted?

Though at times they can bring a sense of discomfort, emotions are truly a gift. They motivate what we do and how we do it. They influ-ence how we react and respond in any given situation. They signal our brain, telling the rest of our body what to do next. So much of our decision making is informed by our emotions because God gave us emotions to assess a situation and respond accordingly.

Imagine if that evening we pulled up to our house, and there was an actual intruder inside. The power of emotional response is that it alerts our body that something is wrong and that we need to act fast. A signal is sent to our brain that prepares the rest of our body to be vigilant, aware, and to get ready to run. Scientists and psychologists call this the "fight, flight, or freeze" response, and it's thanks to our sympathetic system that we have such a flash flood of chemicals rushing to our brain. Those chemicals give us a rapid reaction time to stressful or dangerous situations.

Our sympathetic system is part of our autonomic nervous system, and it's the part of our body that's in charge of sending those response chemicals at the proper time. It's not a system that we naturally control. Things happen automatically. Without our voluntary control, our autonomic nervous system regulates our heart rate, pupil dilation, blood pressure, body temperature, and even our digestive system.[1] We pull up to our house and see a potential intruder—our eyes get wide, our heart rate spikes, we start to sweat, and then we make a run for it. But is it possible for this system to signal us that there's danger when there really isn't? Is it possible for us to feel signs and symptoms of emotional distress, when really we're safe, healthy, and secure?

I think the clear answer to that, based on our interaction with Mary, is yes! Our emotions can lead us astray. We thought there was an intruder, and everything seemed to point in that direction, so our bodies naturally responded. Our emotions responded to a situation, but the response wasn't accurate. That's because our emotions are not all powerful or all knowing. They can't see the full picture. Had they known that there was a harmless 90-year-old lady looking around for a frying pan, they wouldn't have responded the way they did. But they didn't know because our emotions aren't meant to know everything. They're meant to simply respond.

Sometimes our emotions respond to things that aren't accurate because they don't always have the full story. Though our emotions are meant to be a guide—to give us direction and perspective—they aren't meant to lead the way. They aren't meant to have complete control over us. We need to ultimately learn to have control over them.

> Our emotions aren't meant to know everything. They're meant to simply respond.

There have been many times in my life when my feelings led me astray. Like the time I dated a guy for a year and a half because I felt *secure*, even though he wasn't good for me. Or the time I dyed my hair orange because it made me feel *confident*, even though, looking back at photos, I seriously resembled Mufasa from *The Lion King*. But sometimes, feelings can lead us astray in more significant ways. Like the time I almost cancelled a huge speaking engagement—the opportunity to share the message of healthy relationships with thousands of people—because I felt *paranoid* that something terrible was going to happen to my kids if I left. Let me give you some other examples from people I've counseled over the years whose feelings led them astray:

- The woman who left a secure marriage because she felt *unhappy*.
- The girl who stopped going to her college classes because she felt *incompetent*.
- The man who quit his job because he felt *incapable*.
- The boy who skipped basketball tryouts because he felt *doubtful*.
- The young mom who numbed herself with wine because she felt *overwhelmed*.
- The pastor who got lost in pornography because he felt *unworthy*.

Feelings—if not kept in check—can wreak havoc in our lives. Emotions are meant to signal us, but they are not meant to lead us.

Jesus Was Emotional

I love looking at Scripture through the lens of emotional health—especially the characteristics of Jesus. We often describe Jesus as a leader, savior, teacher, and healer. But how often do we see Him as a feeler? Someone who felt and experienced human emotion. He was fully God, yet fully man, which meant He experienced the entire spectrum of emotional colors. Scripture points to the many emotions that Jesus experienced during His time on earth—complete emotional experience yet paired with complete self-control. Some sources have identified 39 emotions that Jesus felt during His 33 years on this earth.[2] Those emotions range from frustration (Matthew 17:14-20), to sorrow (Isaiah 53:3), to fear (Hebrews 5:7), to shame (Hebrews 12:2), to disgust (John 2:13-17), to empathy (John 19:25-27), and to distress (Mark 14:33). Jesus felt, expressed, dealt with, and interacted with so many emotions in a healthy way. And that's only referring to the emotions that have been referenced in Scripture, which we know is only a glimpse of the full picture (John 21:25). If we want to get an understanding of a healthy emotional response, there's no better gauge than when we look at some of the feelings Jesus experienced as well as how He *responded* to those feelings.

> Though our emotions are meant to be a guide—to give us direction and perspective—they aren't meant to lead the way.

The Joy of Jesus

"If you keep my commands," Jesus said, "you will remain in my love, just as I have kept my Father's commands and remain in his love. I have told you this so that my joy may be in you and that your joy may be complete" (John 15:10-11). Jesus experienced joy. But more meaningful is knowing that doing God's will gave Jesus *joy*. Not only that, but He wants us to experience that same kind of joy. Hebrews 12:2 tells us that the reason He endured the pain of the cross, was because of the *joy* set before Him—the joy of being able to share life eternal with me and with you. What brings joy to the heart of Jesus is moving toward God and bringing us along with Him.

When I read these passages and reflect on the *joy* of Jesus, I have to admit I'm challenged to consider the things that bring me joy when held up to the measuring stick of the things that brought Jesus joy. I can find joy in a sandwich. Joy in a new outfit. Joy in making money. Joy in being successful. Joy in being outdoors. Joy in accomplishment. Joy in writing a new book. I'm not saying it's wrong to find joy in these things, but my conviction stems from how far away my joys can wander from the heart of Jesus. If I follow my emotions only toward the things that bring me joy, I can find myself wandering into dangerous territory because sometimes the things that bring me joy fail to see the big picture of God's kingdom. Does my heart find joy in bringing people toward the Father? It's good to find joy in the things God has given us, but it's even better to find joy in God Himself and in the pursuit of moving my heart and the heart of others in His direction. I want my delight to come from simply being with Him, following Him, serving Him, and leading others to Him (Psalm 37:4).

The passage in Luke 15:5-6 is a clear example of the joy that Jesus possesses as He talks about the shepherd and his response to the lost sheep that has been found. "When he finds [the sheep], he joyfully puts it on his shoulders and goes home. Then he calls his friends and neighbors together and says, 'Rejoice with me; I have found my lost sheep.'" What brings your heart joy? And how do those things compare to the things that bring joy to the heart of Jesus?

The Sorrow of Jesus

In Luke 19:41, we get a glimpse of the sorrow and sadness Jesus felt as He approached the city of Jerusalem and "wept over it." His heart was broken for the sins and struggles of His people. Jesus found joy in people moving toward the heart of the Father, but He felt sorrow—deep sadness—when they wandered away. His heart broke for those who didn't know the Father.

Jesus also felt sorrow at the impact of sin—which He knew would ultimately lead to death. When He found out that His friend Lazarus had died, Scripture tells us that His spirit was moved, and He was deeply troubled:

> When Jesus saw her weeping, and the Jews who had come along with her also weeping, he was deeply moved in spirit and troubled. "Where have you laid him?" he asked.
>
> "Come and see, Lord," they replied.
>
> Jesus wept (John 11:33-35).

Jesus understood the feeling of sorrow and sadness. He experienced the sting of loss. I know this passage is often cited as a meaningful reminder that Jesus cried tears of sorrow. He knows the pain of loss the way we know the pain of loss. He knows what it feels like to be gutted with sadness and deeply moved by sorrow. You don't have to feel alone in your sorrow and grief and loss because Jesus knows, feels, and understands.

But we have much to learn from what Jesus did next. The "next step" is so vital for us in understanding how to deal with our own grief, loss, and sorrow. What was *His* "response" to sorrow? What did He do after He wept? I wondered if maybe there was something in this passage that could point us to a proper emotional response when we're feeling the sting of sadness and the deep struggle of sorrow. And sure enough, there it was, clear as day. So clear, that I wondered how I'd missed it so many times before.

"Then Jesus looked up and said, 'Father, I thank you that you have heard me,'" (John 11:41). His first response was to thank the Father. His *first* response after sorrow was gratitude: "Father, I thank You." I know for certain that my first response to sorrow and sadness in my past has not immediately been gratitude. Gratitude has usually been the farthest thing from my mind when I am deeply troubled. I'm slowly learning to move my heart in that direction, but usually, things like distraction or venting or numbing or avoiding get the best of me before I can respond with gratitude. But what if we were to choose to respond to sorrow and sadness with a heart of gratitude—gratitude for who God is and what He means to us, just like Jesus did? "Thank You, God, that You hear us, that You see us, that You know us. Thank You that You listen and come near and don't leave us in our sorrow alone." An emotionally healthy reaction to sadness brings us nearer to God.

The Exhaustion of Jesus

Have you ever felt burned out? Tired? Exhausted? Unable to handle all the pressure that life has thrown your way? John 4:6 reveals to us that even Jesus grew weary physically and emotionally. He was surrounded by needy people and was followed around relentlessly with requests for help and healing. But how did Jesus respond to weariness and exhaustion? He responded with limits. He responded with boundaries. He responded by making sure to fill Himself up so that He could continue pouring out to others. In order to get filled, we first have to acknowledge our emptiness. Jesus, though fully God, allowed Himself to be subject to the limitations of man (Philippians 2:6-7). He felt fatigue, and He responded accordingly. He pulled away from people in exchange for time with God. He made the time and effort to connect with the one thing that could fill Him up: the Father. Luke 5:16 tells us that "Jesus often withdrew to lonely places and prayed."

How do you respond to your emotional exhaustion? How do you react to that signaling in your body that you have reached maximum

> An emotionally healthy reaction to sadness brings us nearer to God.

capacity? Do you ignore it and push through? Do you keep doing more and hope that the feeling just goes away on its own? Do you try to escape or maybe fill yourself up with things like shopping or drinking or eating—things that can't actually fill you up emotionally? Or do you go to the Father? Do you set boundaries and limits around your life and acknowledge that the signal of exhaustion is telling you that you need to be filled? Take some time away, alone, to connect with the One who can fill you up to overflowing.

The Anger of Jesus

The predominant times we see Jesus angry in Scripture are when He was interacting with people who were leading others astray. In Matthew 23:33, we see Jesus's bold and angry response to religious hypocrisy: "You snakes!" He cries. "You brood of vipers! How will you escape being condemned to hell?" Another passage in Scripture depicting the anger of Jesus is John 2:13-17:

> When it was almost time for the Jewish Passover, Jesus went up to Jerusalem. In the temple courts he found people selling cattle, sheep and doves, and others sitting at tables exchanging money. So he made a whip out of cords, and drove all from the temple courts, both sheep and cattle; he scattered the coins of the money changers and overturned their tables. To those who sold doves he said, "Get these out of here! Stop turning my Father's house into a market!" His disciples remembered that it is written: "Zeal for your house will consume me."

The corruption of what was happening in the temple filled Jesus with anger. He sees dishonesty and exploitation, and it makes Him mad. Jesus's anger leads to an emotional response: He calls out hypocrisy and challenges corruption. His anger leads Him to action. But not just any action! Actions that bring truth to lies, justice to injustice, and right to wrongs. Which begs us to ask the question: What kinds of things bring us to fury and anger? Do we find ourselves filled with more anger when the lady in front of us on the highway is driving slower than a horse and buggy (I live in Amish-town, so I have a real-time comparison), or when we see the exploitation of the poor and vulnerable? Do we get angrier when we feel misunderstood by others, or at our own hypocrisy and double standards that cause others to misunderstand our God? It's important to take inventory of our anger, what's really fueling it deep down, and assess whether or not our anger leads us to a beneficial and proper action.

The Compassion of Jesus

Matthew 9:36 tells us that when Jesus "saw the crowds, he had compassion on them, because they were harassed and helpless, like sheep without a shepherd." Oh, the compassion of Jesus! Of all the emotions Jesus displays, His compassion is the one that moves me the most. His heart for the hurting—His ability to feel for those who are suffering and to see those in need. Whether compassion for someone who was struggling from a physical illness or an emotional struggle as a result of their personal sin—Jesus felt compassion, and then He stopped and saw people where they were (Matthew 9:20-22; John 8:1-11).

I want to respond to the emotion of compassion the way Jesus did. Not only do I want to feel compassion for people, but I want to stop—to see people where they are. I don't want to be so busy that I overlook the reality that God can use me to bring hope and healing to the world the way He did. The beautiful thing about compassion is it's an emotion that's for all of us, not just for Jesus. It's one of the only emotions that invites us out of the walls of our own experience and into another's experience. It's an emotion that helps us to feel for others, not just for ourselves. It connects us to the world around us, when we can often be so self-absorbed in our own world. What if we were more in tune to compassion? What if we took the time to stop, see the needs, and do what we could to meet them? I wonder how such an emotional response would change us—would change the world.

The Agony of Jesus

The night before Jesus was crucified was filled with gut-wrenching agony: "Being in anguish, he prayed more earnestly, and his sweat was like drops of blood falling to the ground," (Luke 22:44). He was in so much emotional distress that it triggered an actual physical response. Do you remember earlier we talked about the autonomic response of the body? Here, in the depiction of Jesus sweating blood, we get a glimpse of His humanity and even His autonomic response to distress and deep suffering. There's a rare condition known as hematidrosis when small blood vessels in the skin break open and begin to bleed. The blood then gets funneled into hair follicles or sweat glands and comes out in the form of sweat and blood. As one writer puts it, "Doctors don't know exactly what triggers hematidrosis, in part because it's so rare. They think it could be related to your body's 'fight or flight' response."[3]

His emotions were telling Him to run. But He stayed. His feelings were telling Him to get to safer ground, but instead, He subjected Himself to danger because He knew that the suffering would bring salvation. He knew that His emotions couldn't always be trusted, but His God could always be trusted. "Father, if you are willing, take this cup from me; yet not my will, but yours be done" (Luke 22:42). Friends, if you hear nothing else in this book, hear this: *Jesus stayed for you.* He stayed, even when everything inside Him told Him to run. He trusted His God more than He trusted His feelings because of His deep love for you and for me. He submitted to the cross and willingly gave His life so that we could have power over sin and power over death and power in this life. He stayed, when everything inside of Him told Him to run. And because He stayed, so can we. Because with confidence, we too can declare that though our feelings can't always be trusted, our God can always be trusted.

> Jesus knew His emotions couldn't always be trusted, but His God could always be trusted.

God Is More Real than My Reality

After I had that panic attack on a safari bus, a surge of emotions began impacting my life. Over the following year, my emotions slowly started controlling me, instead of me being in control of my emotions. Physical sickness led to feelings of anxiety. For example, I would be at home making lunch for the kids when, suddenly, I would feel light-headed. I had been so aware of the scary and uncomfortable symptoms during my panic attack that I was afraid it was going to happen again. Any sense of feeling "out of the norm" would send me spiraling into anxiety. Whether it was a headache, fatigue, or anything else that made me feel a little "off," my autonomic system would respond with the fight-or-flight response: My heart rate would rise, my body would heat up, I would begin sweating, and my anxiety would skyrocket. I had to learn a very important lesson: My emotions couldn't always be trusted.

Just because I felt afraid didn't mean there was something to fear.

Just because you feel lonely doesn't necessarily mean you're really alone.

Just because you feel shame doesn't mean there's something to be ashamed of.

Just because you feel guilt doesn't mean you've done something wrong.

Sometimes, our feelings are responding to their own perception of reality—which isn't always real. Like our frightened response to Mary snooping around our house. Sometimes, reality isn't what our emotions are telling us. We've got to get to a place where we learn to trust that God is more real than our reality.

> Just because I felt afraid didn't mean there was something to fear.

My emotional responses eventually got so bad that I had to sit at the end of the row at church because I was afraid of having an episode of panic. Going through tunnels on road trips would heighten my anxiety because I felt like I couldn't escape if something happened—that same feeling I had

felt on that safari bus. I started feeling more and more claustropho-
bic. I didn't schedule any travel or speaking engagements during those
few months because I just couldn't imagine being stuck on an airplane.
What if it happened again? What if I couldn't escape it?

I'm thankful for the gift of counseling, and specifically in this case,
for God's gift of allowing me to *be* a counselor. One clinical connection
I was able to make was that what I was experiencing in the present was
actually rooted in past trauma. My body was remembering and then
overcompensating for some traumatic experiences I had been through
just a few short years ago. Experiences that I'd never really had a chance
to process, to deal with, and to interpret in a healthy way. But all of
this took a while to unfold and understand. I didn't make the connections right away.

One time, a few short months after my first panic episode, I woke
up at 4 a.m. with serious heart palpitations. My heart rate spiked to
over 140 beats per minute while I was just lying there in my bed. That,
paired with something suspicious that had come up in my blood work
from the day before, prompted the on-call doctor to recommend I
head to the emergency room. So, John and I drove over in the middle
of the night and spent four hours in the emergency room, all to find
out there was absolutely nothing wrong with me physically. The CT
scan trumped the blood work and showed me to be in perfect health.
Which is great news...unless you're trying to figure out what on earth is
making you feel so crummy, only to realize there's nothing wrong with
you outside of an overactive stress response.

We have a tendency to really underestimate the power of our emotions. The ER doctors sent me home saying that there was nothing
wrong and hoped that would make me feel better. But it didn't. The
only thing that made me feel better was when I was able to make the
connection that my emotions had hijacked my body, and my anxiety
was causing me to experience actual physical symptoms. But now—
now it was time to take control back. I was resolved that I wouldn't let
my emotions dictate my life because God was more real than my reality,

and He would give me the wisdom and courage I needed to get back to a place of health.

That year brought a series of things to help bring me back to a place of emotional control, including meeting with wise doctors, setting boundaries around my life, stopping one medication (birth control) and starting a new one (an antidepressant), as well as my decision to invite my former mentor and supervisor, Dr. Hamon, into my life to counsel me and join me on the process of working through my past trauma and current emotional struggles. If counselors don't get counseling for themselves, then how on earth can we recommend it to others?

He and I talked through many important aspects of the mind-body connection, and per his area of expertise, he helped give me such a better understanding of the emotional response—what is actually happening in my body that triggers anxiety, as well as how to deal with it. I'll be sure to cover all of those lessons later on in the coming sections about the mind-body connection and trauma, and about the different parts of the brain and how they impact our physical response. But for now, I want to reiterate the most important truth that he said to me during our times together: *God is more real than your reality*. Yes, that beautiful truth I wrote earlier came from him, and it has become such a big part of my mantra in life.

Feelings can't always be trusted. We have to keep them in check, keep them in line, and keep them in balance. We have to learn to identify them, to express them, and to deal with them in healthy ways. Our feelings can *feel* so real that often they can paralyze or confuse us. They can cause us to doubt ourselves or even prevent us from moving forward or engaging out of fear, worry, frustration, shame, or anxiety. We've got to get comfortable with feeling what we feel but then recognizing that God is bigger than our emotions. I could trust His Word, His promises, and His presence. I could trust in His healing, His strength, and His plan for my life. I could believe without a shadow of a doubt that no matter what I was going through, God was going to take the pieces of my life—including my emotions—and work them all together for good: the anxious pieces, the sorrowful pieces, the joyful pieces, and everything in between (Romans 8:28).

How to Let Your Emotions Control You

How can we keep our feelings in check and in balance? Well, let's start with what we shouldn't do and talk through the things that will give your feelings power over you instead of the other way around.

The worst thing we can do for our emotions is to simply ignore them. As I mentioned in chapter 1, when we ignore or repress our emotions, the pressure begins to build underneath the surface, which eventually leads to an emotional rupture of uncontrolled emotion. At this point, your emotions are controlling you and not the other way around. Think of someone you know who tends to have "emotional explosions" throughout life. Maybe you think of your father, who would lash out in anger, or that coworker who eventually gets so fed up she shouts obscenities she can't take back. I think of an acquaintance of mine who had a consistent habit of calling me up in a complete panic, usually around 2 a.m., when she felt overwhelmed with life.

Most of us can probably think of someone we know or have interacted with who seemed to be controlled by their emotions. But maybe, just maybe, the person you're thinking about is yourself. Maybe you are the one who feels controlled by your emotions, and rather than releasing the pressure in healthy ways, you find your emotional time bomb unexpectedly exploding during different stages of your life. Maybe you've lashed out in rage at your children, or screamed empty threats of divorce to your spouse, or lost your temper at work to the point of almost losing your job. Unexpressed emotions will eventually make their way to the surface of your life.

The second thing we can do to let our emotions control us is to never question our emotions and simply respond to them as though they're infallible. To trust your emotions *too much* is just as unhealthy as ignoring them altogether. Emotions are just a signal. They're not Scripture, yet far too often we take them and believe them as though they are God's infallible Word. So, if we shouldn't totally ignore them, and we shouldn't accept them without question, what's the best response? As with most things in life, the best response comes with balance.

How to Take Control of Your Emotions

The first two steps to taking control of our emotions would be the exact opposite of the things we do to allow our emotions to control us. First and foremost, in order to take control of our emotions, we need to *acknowledge our emotions.* In chapter 1, we talked about the importance of being aware of our many different emotions, and that's precisely the first step to controlling our emotions. We've got to know what's going on inside in order to be able to deal with it. We have to learn to pay attention to our emotional world.

One man who did a remarkable job of paying attention to his emotional life was King David. He was so in tune to how he was feeling, and the Psalms are full of emotional colors to prove it. In fact, you can find entire charts online of the many emotions expressed in the book of Psalms. David understood, felt, and expressed emotions from distress and sorrow all the way to gratitude and adoration. He had a deep self-awareness and remarkable insight into what was going on underneath the surface. Whoever says that men aren't good at emotional expression needs to spend some time studying the psalms of David. Take a moment to read through some of these verses from Psalms (emphasis added), looking for the emotion expressed and noting the deep awareness:

- "Answer me when I call to you, my righteous God. Give me relief from my *distress*; have mercy on me and hear my prayer" (Psalm 4:1).

- "In *peace* I will lie down and sleep, for you alone, Lord, make me dwell in safety" (Psalm 4:8).

- "Have mercy on me, Lord, for I am *faint*; heal me, Lord,

for my bones are in *agony*. My soul is in deep *anguish*. How long, LORD, how long?" (Psalm 6:2-3).

- "I am *worn out* from my groaning. All night long I flood my bed with weeping and drench my couch with tears. My eyes grow weak with *sorrow*; they fail because of all my foes" (Psalm 6:6-7).

- "I will give thanks to you, LORD, with all of my heart; I will tell of all your wonderful deeds. I will be *glad* and *rejoice* in you" (Psalm 9:1-2).

- "How long must I wrestle with my thoughts and day after day have *agony* in my heart?" (Psalm 13:2).

- "But I trust in your unfailing love; my heart *rejoices* in your salvation" (Psalm 13:5).

- "Therefore, my heart is *glad* and my tongue *rejoices;* my body will also rest *secure*...You make known to me the path of life; you will fill me with *joy* in your presence" (Psalm 16:9,11).

- "I *love* you, LORD, my strength" (Psalm 18:1).

- "My heart leaps for *joy*, and with my song I praise him" (Psalm 28:7).

- "When I felt *secure,* I said, 'I will never be shaken'" (Psalm 30:6).

- "Why, my soul, are you *downcast*? Why so *disturbed* within me? Put your hope in God, for I will yet praise him, my Savior and my God" (Psalm 43:5).

The list could go on for pages because the psalms are bursting with emotions—deep, beautiful emotions—and an incredible awareness of those emotions ranging from ecstasy to agony. Isn't it interesting, then, that such an emotional and passionate man would be titled as a man after God's own heart (Acts 13:22)? His heart was reflective of God's heart: a God of passion and emotion—yet, a God with complete control of those passions and emotions. There's something remarkably hopeful about knowing that my God knows, understands, and feels what I feel, yet that these emotions are not meant to control me, I'm meant to be controlled by His Spirit.

Which leads us to the second thing we need to do in order to take control of our emotions: We need to *question our emotions.* We have to line our emotions up to the measuring stick of truth, rather than the measuring stick of experience. Because what we *feel* experientially isn't always based on truth. Sometimes, it's based on our past; sometimes, it's based on the lies we've believed; sometimes, it's based on the hurts we've experienced; yet sometimes, it's based on truth. We can't dismiss our emotions, but we also can't take them at their word. We have to question what we're feeling and make sure it lines up to the reality of what we know to be true based on God's Word.

When I think about a time I was feeling so completely overwhelmed, my first thought goes to the time period after the birth of my first child. I shared with you a little about my journey with postpartum depression, but the immense feelings of overwhelm just felt so real. I felt incapable, inadequate, unworthy, and extremely guilty. My feelings *screamed* at me that I couldn't do this. I couldn't handle this. I wasn't made for this. But that was the farthest thing from the truth. When I held my feelings up to the measuring stick of God's Word and who He said I was, I realized that my emotions were real—but they weren't true. I was experiencing real feelings that were impacting my body in real ways, but the feelings I was experiencing weren't rooted in truth. And that is the difference that we need to understand. Your emotions are real, but they aren't always true. What's true is God's Word declared over your life. What's true is your identity in Christ. What's true is that in your weakness, Christ's strength is made perfect. What's true is the Holy Spirit at work in your life and in your situation. What's true is that God promises to take every detail and work it together for your good. His truth supersedes what we feel.

But that doesn't mean we ignore our emotions. We're not spiritual people because we ignore our emotions—remember, all that does is make us unhealthy people. My hard and difficult emotions during that season of my life were a signal to me that something needed to change, that something was wrong, that something was not as it should be. My emotions were the "check engine" light coming up to warn me that my car was on the verge of breaking

> Your emotions are real, but they aren't always true.

down if I didn't get some maintenance. They were real (that something is wrong, and I need to deal with it), but they weren't based on truth (because I am worthy, capable, and made for this). My feelings were a signal, but they weren't Scripture.

Thankfully, I was able to identify my triggers and patterns, stay rooted in God's truth, and recognize that these feelings weren't accurately reflecting who I was—but they did point to the reality that I needed help. Help with my house, help with my kids, and help with my emotions. My mom moved in for a few weeks during that hard season to help me get back to health emotionally and physically. I was able to get the physical help I needed as well as focus on sleeping better, eating better, and decreasing the stress in my life until the postpartum period passed. And you know what? It did pass. Though it often felt like it would never end and that the dark clouds of hard emotions would last forever, eventually, the sunshine of truth came back, and I realized it had been there all along. I just couldn't always see it behind the clouds.

Once you've gotten good at *acknowledging your emotions* and then *questioning your emotions*, the last thing you need to remember so that you can keep control is the power of *expressing your emotions*. When we begin to understand our feelings, healthy people then have to make the choice to express their feelings to the people who matter to them. But emotional expression isn't always easy. It doesn't always come naturally, and it's often not something we learn unless we're taught. It takes practice and understanding.

Express Yourself

It's always interesting to me how many people think they're expressing emotions when they're not expressing emotions at all. When someone asks you how you're feeling, and you respond with, "I'm good," I hope you realize that's not actually emotional expression. *Good* and *bad* are adjectives; they're not feelings. We can have good emotions, and we can have emotions that we perceive as "bad" (although no emotion is bad—uncomfortable maybe, but not bad). But what matters is that we can express what we're feeling rather than lumping it into an ambiguous category like we so often do. If I asked you to tell me about the emotions you've felt this week, could you? If I asked you to tell me about the emotions you've felt just today, could you do that?

If you answered yes, you could identify how you feel and tell me about it, my next question to you is this: *Do you express your emotions?* Because just because you can doesn't mean you do. Do you have people in your life that you talk to about your emotions on a regular basis? Do you engage in activities that allow you to pay attention to your emotions and then express them to others? Do you take part in things that offer you an opportunity to express how you feel to people in your life? And I'm not just talking about sending emojis to your friends in your text messages, I'm talking about heartfelt emotional expression. Just like King David.

One of the best ways to begin the process of emotional expression is through what psychologists and counselors call expressive writing. There have been many studies done noting the link between emotional health and expressive writing, but the earliest research was conducted by Dr. Pennebaker out of the University of Austin. His research showed that writing about your emotions has been linked to better emotional outcomes in dealing with medical illness, stress, and even traumatic experiences.[4] Participants in the study were asked to either write daily about their emotions or about something superficial for fifteen minutes over four consecutive days. The group who was asked to write about their emotions were noted to have fewer visits to the doctor, less use of aspirin to control pain, as well as an overall positive outcome in their long-term evaluation. "The overwhelming majority report that the writing experience was valuable and meaningful in their lives," the researchers concluded.[5] Not only was writing and emotional expression helpful in dealing with difficult emotions and regulating mood long term, but it also helped to increase positive behaviors in participants as well, such as improvements in grades or the quality of relationships. Most interesting to note is that expressive writing also induced not just a positive psychological outcome but a positive *physical* outcome. Health improvements were noted in patients with many physical ailments such as asthma and arthritis, as well as decreases in blood pressure and heart rate. It just goes to show you that the body-mind connection is truly undeniable, and when we take care of one, we automatically influence the other.

Writing helps you organize your thoughts and put into words what you're feeling. It can also play a role in helping you regulate your emotions. Another theory behind why writing is beneficial is because when you've expressed your emotions to yourself, you're more likely to take the next step and express those same emotions to others. As human beings, we have a history of learning through stories. Turning your thoughts, feelings, and experiences into a story through the act of writing frees you up to learn and grow from that story even when—or, should I say, *especially* when—it's your own story.

Consider taking time this week to practice expressive writing. Choose a topic that's important to you—something personal you've experienced in the past or present, or something that's bothering you or causing an increase in emotional distress. Set aside ten to twenty minutes a day for the next four to seven days to write about this topic, continuing along the same topic every day. Don't worry about your grammar, spelling, or punctuation—just let the writing flow, and see what comes to your heart and mind. Write it all down. If you're worried someone might find your writing, tuck it away in a safe place so that you can feel the freedom to really capture what's on your heart and express yourself emotionally.

Getting your emotions on paper is one step in the right direction of getting your emotions under control. Once you've taken some time to practice emotional expression on paper, it's important to consider the next step of learning to express your emotions to someone other than yourself. Consider the type of conversations you're having with your family members, your spouse, or your friends. Do you have people in your life that you feel comfortable expressing your heart to?

I'm a huge advocate of the process of professional counseling because there's nothing as cathartic and healing as therapy. I know I'm biased, being a licensed counselor myself, but I have seen so much healing come from within the space of therapy that I can't even begin to tell you how life changing it can be. I've even experienced the life change for myself, and I know what it can do for you.

Don't DIY

We live in a DIY kind of world, where we really believe we can do everything ourselves. I'm fully aware of that because I'm married to a DIY kind of guy. I think technology is partially to blame because it has ushered us into that mentality as a result of having access to so much information right at our fingertips. When we have a problem with our plumbing, the first thing John will do is check YouTube to see if he can find a solution to the problem. Sometimes he can, but other times he can't, so we end up calling a plumber, and we're always so glad we did. One time the electricity in our house went out, and when we tried checking the fuses and all the troubleshooting he could think of, we still couldn't figure it out, so we ended up calling the electrician. It's a good thing we did because there were some crazy wires crossed down below that could have caused some serious fire damage. There's a limit to what we can DIY. If John tried to DIY his next root canal (which, knowing him, he probably would...I'm not even joking), I would put my foot down.

We can't DIY everything because we don't know everything. There's an element of humility that comes with acknowledging that we can't be good at everything, and we shouldn't be. Our emotional health is no different. We can't just assume it's something we can figure out ourselves. If you find yourself struggling emotionally right now, and maybe you've been struggling for a while, I want you to know there are trained people who can help you get back on the track of emotional health. When your electricity is out, you call the electrician. When your sink is leaking, you call the plumber. When your tooth is decayed, you call the dentist. When you're struggling emotionally, why not call a professional counselor?

As we close this section on emotional health, I want you to take inventory of all the things we have discussed that you *can* do to impact your emotional health: understanding your emotions, identifying your past patterns, acknowledging your present patterns and triggers, learning to express your emotions in a healthy way—but it's also important to acknowledge when you can't. When you've tried time and time again and failed. When the problems seem too big for you to tackle alone. When your past is too dark and daunting. When you're nearing the point of wanting to give up. When it's starting to feel like there's no hope for healing. Remember this: You don't have to do it alone; in fact, you weren't meant to.

> Your heart is valuable, and it's worth the work.

Find a counselor who is a licensed professional counselor but also a Christian. Someone who can guide you toward emotional health in a holistic way. Living intentionally means taking the health of your emotional world seriously. Because your heart is valuable, and it's worth the work. There's no better time to begin this process than today. Right here. Right now.

Here are two options to start the counseling process:

1. You can schedule an online session with me by going to TrueLoveDates.com/store. I can't work with everyone, but I can work with some, and I'm grateful to be able to do what I can to help you on this journey.

2. I also want to introduce you to an online counseling agency made up of Christian licensed counselors. Get matched with a professional counselor in 24 hours and begin the journey of healing: https://getfaithful.com/debra.

Journaling Questions: 5-Minute Emotional Checkup

- Am I usually in control of my emotions, or are my emotions usually in control of me?

- Which of Jesus's emotions do I connect with the most in my own personal life? How do I respond to my emotions, and what can I learn from His responses?

- What is my reaction to the idea that David was emotional and passionate and considered a "man after God's own heart"?

- How would I rate myself with regard to the following areas (10 being the best, 0 being the worst)?

  o Emotional Awareness: I'm good at recognizing what I'm feeling and connecting the dots to how it's impacting me. _____

  o Emotional Questioning: I'm good at realizing my emotions aren't always accurate and responding accordingly. _____

  o Emotional Expression: I'm good at expressing the emotions going on inside of me to the people around me. _____

- What are some ways I can get better at each of the areas listed above?

- Do I tend to try and DIY my own emotional health? How so?

- Is it time to invite a licensed counselor into my journey of emotional health? Why or why not?

- Consider taking a few minutes today to practice expressive writing in your journal, and begin getting in tune to how you feel and what's going on inside of you.

PART 2

Spiritual Health
Getting Real with Your Soul

Love the Lord your God with all your...soul.
LUKE 10:27

4

God Is _____

My View of God

One of the scariest days of my life happened at a psychiatric hospital. I was a young counselor at the time, without much clinical experience. While I was finishing up graduate school, I got a part-time job working at a hospital on a psychiatric floor for children and adolescents, hoping it would help bolster my experience and get me ready for the world of private practice.

My first few weeks on the unit were eye-opening, to say the least. Up until then, the world of counseling and psychology had been mostly confined to my textbooks and research papers. Now, the things I had learned about were literally looking me in the eyes—in the faces of children and teenagers going through serious psychological struggles.

Each day I came into work, I was assigned four to five patients that I would check in with and monitor throughout the day. I don't think I'll ever forget the names and faces of those first few patients. One of the first teenagers I had the great privilege of working with was a 15-year-old girl who was completely catatonic, meaning she was unable to move without assistance. She sat in her chair, staring blankly out at nothing. Physically speaking, there was nothing wrong with her body: no serious disease or illness. But psychologically speaking, she was in turmoil. She had gone through horrific trauma, and it literally paralyzed her—emotionally and physically. My eyes were starting to open to the realities of the importance of mental and emotional health. Eventually, she was able to make significant breakthroughs during her time in the hospital and begin to deal with some of her past trauma. Slowly, over a period of a few months, she was able to regain control of her emotional world—and her physical world followed suit. She was eventually discharged to go home and continue her process of healing.

On my second week of work, I was in put charge of a teenage boy who was displaying psychotic symptoms. Psychotic symptoms are essentially when a person is disconnected from reality. He was struggling with hallucinations—hearing and seeing things that weren't really there. My job was to check in with him a few times a day and fill out an inventory on how he was doing emotionally. One day, I came into his room to find him sitting in his bed, staring blankly at the white wall in front of him. I had my inventory in my hand and began small talking with him, trying to see if I could get him to check in with me on how he was doing. He responded to my questions in one-word answers, without ever breaking his gaze at the wall.

I remember feeling a little nervous, considering it was my second week on the job, and one of my nervous habits is to grab something to twirl between my fingers—sometimes a strand of hair, other times my wedding ring. This time, I lifted my arm up and touched my hand to the pearl earrings I was wearing that day, twisting the earring around as I continued waiting for his responses.

All of a sudden, he glanced over at me. He instantly noticed I was twirling my earring. And within seconds, his demeanor began to change. His body started to tense up, and I could sense him getting uncomfortable. He started breathing faster and faster, and then he locked eyes with me in a cold, dark stare.

"I HATE YOU!" he screamed at me, "YOU HAVE NO IDEA!"

Instantly, I was on high alert. I knew he had gone into another one of his psychotic episodes where he was hearing and seeing things that weren't really there. He was looking at me, but he was also looking past me. And within seconds, he began to unleash all his fury on me—the innocent bystander.

"YOU'RE EVIL!" he raged. "YOU'VE RUINED MY LIFE!"

He got up from his bed and started quickly moving in my direction.

This young man was after me, and I instantly knew I needed to get out of there.

I ran out of the room and pushed a panic button on my pager, calling for a code. In a psychiatric hospital setting, a code is called when you or one of the patients is in danger. All the staff carried pagers with little red buttons, and within seconds after pushing the button, I was surrounded by nurses, counselors, and security guards.

One of the security guards ushered me into the locked nursing station, while they proceeded to calm down the young man and escort him back to his room.

But I was in a state of shock. What had changed in literally seconds that took this young man from peacefully gazing at his wall to furiously coming after me? I couldn't figure it out. Needless to say, for the rest of the week I was assigned to a different patient and was told to stay far away from him until we could figure out what triggered his psychotic episode.

Transference

I wonder if you have any thoughts or theories about what took this young man from 0 to 100? Have you ever found yourself totally triggered by something or someone to the point where your behavior was out of control? What might influence that type of behavior?

As we unpacked this situation at our staff meeting, one thing that came to the surface of what happened was that this young man was "transferring" his anger onto me, but the person he was really furious at was his mother. During his counseling sessions, he revealed bits and pieces about his dysfunctional relationship with his abusive mom—a very proper, unemotional, demanding, critical woman, who—maybe you guessed it—wore pearl earrings. Not only did she wear pearl earrings, but she had a habit of twirling her earrings with her fingers. As soon as he saw me doing that same little gesture, his brain snapped into transference mode. In his mind, I was his mother, and he was unleashing all his anger toward her onto me.

In all honesty, that was truly one of the scariest moments of my life. I was inexperienced and unprepared for that level of rage and fury from a patient. But in the end, it was a valuable teaching moment. In graduate school, I had learned all about a psychological concept called transference. In fact, I had an entire class focused on transference—how to recognize it as well as how to use it to your advantage in the therapy setting. But here I was seeing it happen right before my eyes, in probably the most extreme way I have ever witnessed, even to this day.

Transference is the act of transferring how we feel about something or someone onto an innocent bystander. We take out our hurts, frustrations, anger, sadness, pain, and struggles on someone else. We allow our pain to come to the surface, and then put it on the people around us. Have you ever heard the phrase "hurt people, hurt people"? That is a prime example of transference and how we can take our wounds and end up wounding others.

But not only do we transfer our hurts onto other people. One thing I have observed over the years in the lives of my clients, friends, and family—and also in my own life—is that we also have a tendency of transferring our hurts onto God.

God Is _____

How we see, know, and understand God makes all the difference in how we interact with Him. So much of our view of God, especially in our formative years, is shaped by the people around us. For most of us, the people we spend the most time with in our formative years are our parents or the people who raised us. Without even being aware of it, our view of God was shaped by the interactions we had with our primary caregivers. How they treated us and what they expected of us began to imprint in our hearts and minds who God is and what He's all about—whether or not it's true of Him.

Cindy's Story

"I have a hard time believing that God is a good Father." She spoke the words so directly that I knew there had to be more to her story. "I mean, how can He really be so good, when there is so much pain and hurt in the world? How can He be so good when *I* have experienced so much pain and hurt in my life? Where was God then?"

Cindy was in counseling because she knew she needed to deal with some of her past wounds. Cindy had grown up in an emotionally abusive home, at the hands of an emotionally abusive father who called himself a Christian. Not surprisingly, this experience had not only wounded Cindy, it had also tainted her view of God. How can God be trusted as a good Father, when her own father couldn't even be trusted? How could she even begin to call God her Father, when the word *father* stirred up so much pain in her own life?

Cindy was not only hurt at the hands of her father, she was having a really hard time seeing God outside of the image that had been created out of her experiences: that fathers are incapable of being good, loving, and kind. To her, God was no different. Cindy had transferred her pain onto the face of God—seeing Him as just another man she couldn't trust.

Michael's Story

Michael, on the other hand, grew up without a dad. His dad left their family when Michael was just a toddler, so his single mom was the primary caregiver for most of his formative years. After his father left, his mom went into "control mode." She couldn't control the fact that her husband had walked out on her, so she decided to take control of anything and everything she could control—namely, her children. As Michael describes it, "She went into overdrive mode, controlling everything and anything we did as kids. We couldn't even eat something without her awareness. She was on us all the time, and we really felt like we were being suffocated."

As Michael started to attend youth group in the later years of his life, he was introduced to God and gave his heart to Jesus. But for the next years into his young adulthood, he couldn't help but see God as a control freak. "There's just too many rules to follow. And if you break a rule, you're damned," he noted in one of our times together. "I'm starting to feel suffocated by my own faith."

I couldn't help but notice a theme between how Michael grew up and his present view of God. Could it be that Michael was transferring his past experiences onto the face of God? Could it be that Michael was seeing God through his own personal filter of hurt, rather than through the lens of Scripture?

Your View of God

I wonder if you've seen this concept play out in your own life. I know I've seen it throughout mine. There was a time in my life where I took the value statements of my childhood—the "do more" mentality that I talked about earlier—and transferred that onto my view of God. In my mind, God was proud of me when I accomplished something. The more I did, the more He loved me. But what happens when you can't "do more"? What happens during those times in my life where I had to hit the pause button due to illness, depression, or heck, even a migraine? I remember believing that God must be disappointed in me when I had to stop my "doing."

Until one day when God replaced my view of Him with His truth. He challenged me to stop transferring my false beliefs onto Him and instead see Him for how He has revealed Himself through His Word.

I was in my early twenties when I had this life-changing revelation. You know—when you're reading through Scripture, and it's almost as though God just puts a spotlight on something He wants you to see. I was reading the story of Jesus's baptism. I had read this story so many times before, but this time something stood out to me that never had before.

> As soon as Jesus was baptized, he went up out of the water. At that moment heaven was opened, and he saw the Spirit of God descending like a dove and alighting on him. And a voice from heaven said, "This is my Son, whom I love; with him I am well pleased" (Matthew 3:16-17).

For the first time in my life I saw it: God was pleased with Jesus *before* He had done anything significant. In fact, He hadn't really done *anything* yet. The baptism of Jesus was the absolute start of His ministry journey. Before that, Jesus was just like any other young adult man with regard to His successes. He was a carpenter who made a living by building things, spent time with His family and friends, and lay low in the world of accomplishments. Yet, God looked down on His Son and was *well pleased.* He was pleased because of who Jesus *was* to Him, not because of what Jesus *did* for Him.

My eyes were opened to the reality of how I had transferred so much of my view of God from my childhood. The "work hard" mentality was coming more from what I had experienced and seen rather than from Scripture. I realized then and there that God was pleased with me because of who I was to Him, not because of what I did for Him. I allowed God's Word to replace the false view I had transferred onto God—the view that had turned Him into something that reflected more of my history than His story.

I wonder what—or who—has shaped your view of God. If I asked you to give me a list of words to describe God, what would you say? The average Christian will likely jump to the first good Christian, cookie-cutter answers that come to mind: that God is loving, good, strong, and mighty. But do me a favor and dig a little deeper than that. What do you really believe about God? For most of us, if we're truly honest with ourselves, other words will end up making it onto the list. Because our past has a way of transferring onto our present, even in what we think and believe about God.

Here are some false beliefs that some people have about God. Ask yourself if you hold on to any of these beliefs about who God is:

- Controlling
- Judging
- Vindictive
- Success driven
- Angry
- Ashamed of you
- Fed up
- Distant
- Demanding
- Unfair
- Unforgiving
- Apathetic

Understanding your beliefs about God is so important because your beliefs about God shape your relationship with God and, ultimately, your spiritual health. You've got to take inventory of the things that you've transferred onto God over the years and allow the truth of His Word to overcome the template of your experiences. God wants us to stop seeing Him through the eyes of what others have told us, or through the things

> **Allow the truth of His Word to overcome the template of your experiences.**

that have been done to us. He wants us to see Him for who He says He is and take Him at His Word.

According to the truth of His Word, God is...

- Love (1 John 4:16)
- Miracle working (Galatians 3:5)
- Ever present (Psalm 139:1)
- All knowing (1 John 3:20)
- Father of mercies (2 Corinthians 1:3)
- Mighty to save (Isaiah 63:1)
- The Prince of Peace (Isaiah 9:6)
- Wonderful Counselor (Isaiah 9:6)
- Faithful and True (Revelation 19:11)
- For us (Romans 8:31)
- Our Healer (Isaiah 53:5)
- Rich in mercy (Psalm 136)
- Promise keeper (Psalm 145:13)

My friends, that is just a small glimpse of how God reveals Himself through His Word. Imagine if we could embrace the truth of who He is, rather than the false things we've believed Him to be. How could it impact our life? How would it impact our relationship with Him?

Your View Impacts Your Relationships

The young man I met in the psychiatric hospital had a faulty view of who I was. To him, I was just as evil as his critical, demanding, and abusive mother. As soon as he transferred his wrong beliefs onto me, it changed the entire dynamic of our interaction. What could have been a healing interaction ended up fueling more hurt and pain—all because of false beliefs.

As we enter into this section of the book looking at our spiritual health, I wonder what views might be holding you back from your relationship with God. What might be keeping you from feeling the closeness, intimacy, and connection that God wants to give you?

When we think about spiritual health, our minds often quickly drift to the spiritual checklist of things we're doing *for* God:

- Reading my Bible—Check
- Praying every day—Check
- Going to church—Check
- Staying away from sin—Check

But keeping that superficial checklist is not actually a reflection of the health of our spirits as much as it is a reflection of the health of our schedules and personal discipline. We can *do all those things* and still be spiritually unhealthy because we don't really see God for who He is. Don't get me wrong, I'm not saying that spiritual disciplines such as prayer and reading God's Word aren't important, but the reason we're doing those things reflects more about our spiritual health than the simple fact that we're doing them. If I'm running through my spiritual checklist out of guilt, fear, and shame, am I actually spiritually healthy? If I'm going to church and staying away from sin because I believe I'll be damned if I don't, then do I really see God for who He is?

Spiritual health is freeing because it moves us from seeing God for who we think He is to seeing Him for who He reveals Himself to be through His Word. And when we begin to really embrace that God is rich in mercy and forgiveness, full of love and grace, quick to forgive, slow to anger, and ultimately that *He is for us*—we begin to truly piece together the reality that the "spiritual checklist" is not something we do for Him, but rather, something we do for ourselves. Doing those things doesn't make you spiritually healthy, but when you're spiritually healthy, you often do those things.

When my husband was in medical school many years ago, a young man from the community—who had absolutely no connection to the medical school or local hospital—decided to play a little prank. Doctors and medical students wear white coats as part of their uniform, so this young man somehow got his hands on a white coat and decided to spend the entire week in the hospital acting like he was a doctor. He wore this white coat and walked around the hospital visiting patients and interacting with people all day long. He would come to "work" every day, and he would blend right in. Looking at his white coat, people just assumed he was a medical doctor, which is why this situation lasted much longer than it should have, until he was finally caught and seriously reprimanded. Doctors wear white coats, but wearing a white coat doesn't make you a doctor.

The same goes with spiritual health: Just because you run through your list doesn't mean you're spiritually healthy. Spiritually healthy people display spiritually healthy disciplines, but what makes you spiritually healthy is not the list of the disciplines you do, but more so, why you do those things and what's going on underneath the surface. When we enter a true and healthy relationship with Jesus, our motivation begins to come out of a place of love and respect for who He is, rather than fear, guilt, and shame. I love how the book of Romans puts it, reminding us that what really leads to life change is seeing God for who He is: "He has been very kind and patient, waiting for you to change, but you think nothing of his kindness. Perhaps you do not understand that God is kind to you so you will change your hearts and lives" (2:4 NCV).

"Perhaps you do not understand" who God really is. Perhaps you don't see His vast kindness, His ferocious love, His deep mercy. Because when you get a full glimpse of His love for you, it begins to change you from the inside out. When you get a glimpse of all He's done for you, it reminds you of what you mean to Him. When you get a glimpse of how much He wants you, to the point where He sent Jesus as a sacrifice so that He could be with *you*, it motivates you to move toward spiritual health. When you see Him for who He is, you're drawn to Him like nothing else in this world. King David said it the best when he got a glimpse of God for who He really is: "As the deer pants for streams of water, so my soul pants for you, my God. My soul thirsts for God, for the living God. When can I go and meet with God?" (Psalm 42:1-2).

It was no longer about fulfilling a spiritual checklist for David. It was about a desperate desire, a deep longing, an unquenchable thirst for God like nothing he'd ever felt before. When can I get away to be with You, God? When can I be in Your presence? Because there's nothing else in this world that can fulfill the thirst in my soul but You.

When is the last time you felt that longing, that desire, that unquenchable thirst for God? When you see God for who He really is, it begins to change everything. It transforms your spiritual health starting from the inside out.

Inside-Out Living

When we begin to see God clearly, we also begin to live differently. I've always loved the story of Moses going up Mount Sinai to meet with God. After coming down from the mountain, having seen God for who He really is, Moses had changed—literally. The Bible tells us, "His face was radiant because he had spoken with the LORD" (Exodus 34:29). In fact, his face was so bright that he eventually had to wear a veil over it when he wasn't with God because people were afraid to come close (Exodus 34:30,33).

I love that story because it reminds me that a true encounter with God changes everything. It changes us from the inside out. Not only are we different on the inside, but we also begin to change everything about how we live, act, and behave. We "glow" with a new radiance because we've met with God.

> A true encounter with God changes everything.

In taking inventory of our spiritual health, we've got to ask ourselves how we've changed. What has influenced us on the inside, and how has it impacted us on the outside? God's Word is clear that when we're walking in step with God, we'll be filled with the fruit of His Spirit. This passage in the book of Galatians is so powerful, it's worth memorizing:

> So I say, walk by the Spirit, and you will not gratify the desires of the flesh. For the flesh desires what is contrary to the Spirit, and the Spirit what is contrary to the flesh. They are in conflict with each other, so that you are not to do whatever you want. But if you are led by the Spirit, you are not under the law.
>
> The acts of the flesh are obvious: sexual immorality, impurity and debauchery; idolatry and witchcraft; hatred, discord, jealousy, fits of rage, selfish ambition, dissensions, factions and envy; drunkenness, orgies, and the like. I warn you, as I did before, that those who live like this will not inherit the kingdom of God.
>
> But the fruit of the Spirit is love, joy, peace, forbearance, kindness, goodness, faithfulness, gentleness and self-control. Against such things there is no law. Those who belong to Christ Jesus have crucified the flesh with its passions and desires. Since we live by the Spirit, let us keep in step with the Spirit (5:16-25).

Are you keeping in step with the Spirit? Is your life marked more by the acts of the flesh or the fruit of the Spirit? Because that is one way to really take inventory of the health of your soul. One thing I appreciate about this passage in Galatians is that it gives us a list of harmful behaviors that are "acts of the flesh." I'm a practical person, and so I always appreciate a list of things to "avoid" as well as things to "embrace" when it comes to my spiritual life.

As a relationship counselor, I've spent a lot of time talking about and studying the fruit of the Spirit because so much of the health of our relationships comes down to our personal health. My main message at my relationship advice blog, TrueLoveDates.com, is that healthy people make healthy relationships. The healthier we are, the healthier our relationships will be. One reason I really appreciate Galatians 5 is because it lays out for us the true qualities of health. In essence, it says, "Healthy people look like this." All of those positive qualities listed as the fruit of the Spirit are also the exact qualities you need to engage in a healthy relationship.

So then, what qualities should you avoid? Let's think through what the opposites of the fruit of the Spirit might look like. If healthy people and healthy relationships look like this, then what do unhealthy people and unhealthy relationships look like? I took the opposite trait of each of the fruit of the Spirit, and here's what I came up with:

FRUIT OF THE SPIRIT → *OPPOSITE ACTIONS*

LOVE → *BITTERNESS and HATE*

JOY → *NEGATIVITY and PESSIMISM*

PEACE → *UNCONTROLLED ANXIETY*

PATIENCE → *SHORT FUSE and TEMPER*

KINDNESS → *AGGRESSION*

GOODNESS → *SELFISHNESS and SELF-CENTEREDNESS*

FAITHFULNESS → *LACK OF TRUST and DECEIT*

GENTLENESS → *HARSH and CRITICAL*

SELF-CONTROL → *ADDICTION*

In taking inventory of my spiritual health and the things that are radiating from my life starting from the inside out, I often look back at this list and question which side of the spectrum I'm living out of. Do I approach people with love or bitterness? Am I faithfully representing who I am, or is there a tendency to compromise my honesty? Am I acting out of self-control, or am I allowing addictions to settle into my life in how I'm treating technology, food, and so many other things?

As you look through this list one by one, I want you to ask yourself the same type of questions. Are you living guided by the Spirit or the flesh? Are you motivated by a truthful view of who God is and what He means to you, or are you living out of transference and lies? Because what you believe about God impacts your relationship with God. And your relationship with God impacts every other part of your life.

Spiritual health is not something we stumble upon. It's something we seek. And it starts with looking in, getting things right from the inside out. God is _____. The answer to that has the power to change everything.

Journaling Questions: 5-Minute Spiritual Checkup

- What people or experiences have shaped my view of God?

- What are some words that I have believed about God that are *not* based on truth? How have these false beliefs impacted my relationship with God over the years?

- What are some of the characteristics of God, revealed through His Word, that are most significant to me? (See list on page 105.) How can I allow these *true* characteristics to reignite my love and desire for God?

- When I look at the fruit of the Spirit, which ones on the list are the *least* evident in my life? What opposite traits do I tend to see most often in my life?

- Write out a prayer asking God to bring healing and replace any lies you might be holding onto with His truth. Ask Him to exchange the actions of the flesh for the fruit of His Spirit.

Hello, My Name Is _____

My View of Self

Each time I saw her, she looked less and less like herself.

Which is unfortunate because Kelly was a beautiful young woman. She was one of those people who had a natural glow to her. In fact, she's probably someone most women would envy because she didn't need makeup to accentuate her naturally beautiful features. Her thick eyebrows framed her perfect almond-shaped eyes, which sat right above her high and symmetrical cheekbones. Her dark hair fell around her face and came down to her chin—a tiny chin with a little dimple that added a sense of innocence and kindness to her smile. She was truly a beautiful young woman, but unfortunately, that's not the way she saw herself. In fact, Kelly had undergone surgery after surgery for one simple reason: She hated how she looked. And with each surgery, she began to look less and less like herself. But no matter how many cosmetic surgeries she endured, she still couldn't get herself to see her face as beautiful. All she could see were her perceived flaws. She felt hideous, and nothing she did could change how she viewed herself.

Kelly suffered from Body Dysmorphic Disorder (BDD)—a disorder that distorts the way people see themselves. It shares some similar traits with other mental health disorders such as obsessive-compulsive disorder (OCD) and eating disorders. All of these diagnoses come in the form of some sort of rumination or obsessions. But in the case of an eating disorder, the obsessions revolve around body image on a whole, and in the case of BDD, the obsession revolves around one specific body part that a person can't stop fixating on. For Kelly, it was her face. For different people, the fixation can find its way to specific parts of the body, such as the nose, thighs, skin, breasts, or hair. But the bottom line is that a person with BDD sees a part of their body as intolerable and something they desperately need to find a way to fix. According to a recent study, nearly 2 percent of people struggle with BDD.[1] It's a disorder that causes a significant amount of distress in both men and women. It usually begins to manifest itself in the teen or young adult years and is often a chronic disorder.

I have witnessed horror stories of the things BDD has caused people to do—from taking a hammer to their nose, to spending thousands of dollars on plastic surgery after plastic surgery, to withdrawing from society altogether. People who suffer from BDD have a tendency to isolate themselves socially because of their perceived flaws. One study reported that in adolescents diagnosed with BDD, over 60 percent of them were not attending school or only attending sporadically.[2] People with BDD often don't want to be around people for fear that others will also fixate on their physical flaws. Their fixation impacts their entire life. But the most interesting thing about BDD is that the fixation is always rooted in a lie—a lie about who they believe themselves to be.

I've worked with people diagnosed with BDD who had no physical flaws from my perspective, but the flaw was in how they perceived themselves. The fixation wasn't based on reality, but rather, on a label they had placed on themselves or that someone else had placed on them—that they are "ugly," or that "something is wrong with them"—a label that they began to believe and then live out of over the years.

How we view ourselves can have a huge impact on our personal health. But the labels that we carry, the words that tell us who we think we are, can often be laced with lies and deceit. And if we're not aware of the labels we're carrying, we end up living out of those labels, which most often means living based on the lies, rather than based on the truth.

The Labels We Carry

One of the most powerful stories I ever heard came in the form of an email from a young woman from India, with the subject line "Healed by an American." A subject line like that will really get your attention. In her email, she told me of the tremendous hardships she had endured through her life. She was born with a physical deformity, which is shamed in her society. Not only that, but she experienced a combination of physical, sexual, and emotional abuse that led her to believe the lies that she heard telling her she was unworthy, useless, deformed, and incapable. Rejected by her own family and questioning her very worth, she felt like her life wasn't worth living. Not only did she begin to question her own existence, but also the existence of God. One evening, when things felt like they couldn't get any darker, she tried to take her own life. But fear held her back because she just couldn't get herself to do it.

Shortly after that dark evening, during a leisurely search on the Internet one evening, she happened upon TrueLoveDates.com. She read every article she could get her hands on and devoured the content:

> After reading each and every article, I began to understand
> how toxic and sick my life is. I have spent a good deal of
> my life wallowing in self-hatred and resenting just about

everything in and around my life. I was just good at hating
and resenting and giving everyone around me a hard time.

After experiencing your writings, I took inventory of my
life, like you put it. I decided to let go of some people...You
keep talking about healthy people, healthy relationships.
My life is far from healthy. But I want to try and I start by
writing you this very long email.

What had changed from one day to the next? One thing: the lies she
was believing about herself. She went from "wallowing" in self-hatred
and the labels that told her she was unworthy and incapable, to believing that she had something to offer the world—and that maybe, just
maybe, God had a plan and purpose for her life:

I am far from being physically okay but I do want to have
the courage to show love and compassion towards the
physically handicapped or someone with needs greater
than mine. I want to develop a good relationship with God,
He is my creator after all, and eventually grow more Christ-
like. I want to forgive my parents and everyone who ever
did me wrong. Above all, I am ready to forgive myself...I
have hope. Hope in tomorrow, hope in the future, and
hope in the afterlife.

Reading her email again brings me to tears. Tears of joy and tears of
hope. Things begin to change—better yet, miracles begin to happen—
when we take inventory of what we are believing about ourselves and
begin aligning those beliefs with God's unchanging truth.

Reading a story like the one above, most of us can easily see the vulnerable place she was in and how easy it would be to begin believing
lies about yourself when faced with such difficult circumstances and
surrounded by such an unloving family. But what about you? Your life
may not have been as hard as this young woman's life, but I want you
to consider this question: What labels might you be believing that are
impacting your life?

Black and Blue Buttons

Jeff and his wife came in for counseling one day to deal with conflict that was coming up again and again in their marriage. Anytime his wife asked him to change something, fix something, or deal with something, he would find himself getting angry and upset. He felt like his wife was a nag, and there was always "more" to be done. Nothing he ever did felt like it was good enough for her. One day, they were gardening together in their backyard when she noticed some weeds that he hadn't pulled in the corner.

"Are you going to get those?" she asked innocently.

"Of *course* I'm going to get those!" he screamed. "Do you think I'm that incompetent? Haven't you seen me working hard all day?! Do you have to be such a nag about everything?!"

Something was clearly wrong. And they were feeling stuck. Without either of them realizing it, Jeff's wife had hit a button that caused him to react with a really strong emotional response. I call those our "black and blue buttons."

Have you ever bumped into a table or something that caused a significant bruise? Just the other day, I was hurrying out of our house so I wouldn't be late to an appointment when I got too close to the coat hanger sticking out on the wall, and my shoulder slammed right into it with full force. Let me just say, it hurt like you know what. For the next few days, I had a serious black and blue bruise on my shoulder. When John would come over to give me a hug or rub my shoulder, he'd unintentionally push against the bruise, causing me to react by pulling away and grimacing in pain. He was inflicting pain on an already sore area without even realizing it. He was pressing my black and blue button. And it hurt!

Just like our physical black and blue bruises, we have emotional black and blue bruises as well. Places where someone or something has caused pain in the past and left us with an emotional bruise. So how do we know we have them? All we have to do to find our "black and blue buttons" is look for a strong negative emotional reaction. Anytime you find yourself with a heightened or exaggerated negative emotional response to something, there's a good chance there's a black and blue bruise that you haven't identified. Which brings me back to Jeff's story.

I asked Jeff to try and put into words what he was feeling when his wife "nagged" him.

"It makes me feel like she thinks I'm an incompetent fool!" he said.

"Well, that's not a *feeling*, Jeff. That's a description of what you think your wife believes. Which is a good start, but can you try to identify what you're feeling?" I responded.

"It makes me feel inadequate. Like I'm not good enough," he replied.

Now we were getting somewhere.

I asked Jeff to think back to another time, long before his wife, when he'd felt that deep feeling of inadequacy.

He shook his head a bit and looked down at the floor. Then he started telling me about his relationship with his dad.

> With my dad, it was always his way or the highway. I lived my entire life under his thumb. Nothing I ever did was good enough for him, no matter how hard I tried. I was a good kid, but it didn't seem like I could ever measure up to his standard. I never felt good enough for him, and when I was 16 years old, things came to a head. We had a huge fight, and I ended up leaving home. I haven't had a relationship with my dad since that day. I was never going to be good enough for him.

And with that insightful observation, I watched as Jeff—a big, strong man covered in tattoos—began to weep like a child right there in my office. And if I'm honest, I shed a few tears too. It was remarkable to watch Jeff begin to make the connections of what was really going on underneath the surface. For far too long, he had been carrying the label that told him he "wasn't good enough," and that label was starting to impact his life and his closest relationships.

Jeff had a "black and blue button," an emotional bruise that was causing him severe pain. And anytime his wife got near that button with a request or a critique, she would press up against his bruise without ever realizing it, and he would react. His emotional bruise was the label that he was carrying that told him he wasn't good enough, and as long as he continued to believe that lie, he would continue to struggle.

Tabula Rasa

One of the founding fathers of psychology was a man by the name of John Locke. John Locke theorized the "tabula rasa," which means "blank slate" in Latin. According to Locke, human beings are born with no identity of their own. They're essentially a blank slate. Imagine a giant whiteboard with nothing on it, clear and free of any preconceived ideas. But as we go through life, different people and different experiences begin to put their mark on our blank slate. They begin to give us labels—words that shape what we believe about ourselves.

Some of the labels that people place over our lives are uplifting, affirming, and encouraging. I think of my three children and the intentional words I am speaking over their life every single day in an attempt to shape their identity and what they believe about themselves. But other times, the labels that people place on us are not so kind. They're hurtful, mean, and downright ugly. They're lies—lies that we end up carrying for so long that we begin to believe them and live out of them, even though they aren't true. I think of Jeff and the label that he was carrying—that he was "not good enough." I think of the young woman from India and the label that she was carrying—that she was "unworthy." And then I think of me and you and the labels that have been put on our blank slate by people who have influenced us to believe something about ourselves that isn't true.

Maybe it was the boyfriend who told you that you were ugly.

Or the teacher who convinced you that you would never amount to anything.

Maybe it was the abuser who got you to believe that you were shameful.

Or the coach who caused you to believe that you didn't have what it takes.

Maybe it was the absent father who caused you to believe you weren't worth his time.

Or the critical mother who affirmed that you were just not good enough.

What labels have been placed on you, and how long have you carried those labels?

Hello, My Name Is _____

Our identity is not only crucial to our emotional health, but it's vital for our spiritual health because a large part of being a spiritually healthy person is found in being able to see ourselves the way that God sees us. Because how we see ourselves influences everything, including how we relate to God. Seeing ourselves how God sees us means seeing ourselves through the lens of truth—a lens that hasn't been tainted by the sin and struggle of this world. A lens that hasn't been dimmed by pain and trauma and difficult experiences. Seeing ourselves through the lens of how God sees us opens us up to seeing truthfully. And it's only by seeing the truth that we can really be set free (John 8:32).

It's amazing how many labels that we carry without ever realizing it. Whenever I am asked to speak at a church or college or conference, I'm usually invited to come and speak about healthy relationships. So, it often comes as a little bit of a surprise when I begin by teaching about becoming healthy while standing alone. But to me, they are one and the same. I start by talking about healing from our past, and then I move into talking about healing of our present—specifically, healing in what we believe about ourselves. Because what we believe about ourselves determines the kind of relationships we believe we deserve.

> What we believe about ourselves determines the kind of relationships we believe we deserve.

During the portion of the talk where I focus on identity, I pull out those red labels that say "Hello, My Name Is" on them. They're meant to be used to write your name on, but I ask the audience to keep them blank until I explain what I want them to do with those labels.

Eventually, I ask them to do something very brave and courageous. I challenge them to take an empty label and think about one word— one label—that someone has spoken over their life that *isn't* God's truth. Then I ask them to write down their word, and during a time of prayer where eyes are closed and heads are bowed, I ask them to bring up their labels to the "Tabula Rasa" I have on the stage—usually a big whiteboard.

After everyone returns to their seats, we have a moment of silence, and then I take a few minutes to read the labels aloud one by one. Friends, I can't even tell you how hard it is for me to read through those labels. One hundred percent of the time I well up, with tears streaming down my face, my voice choked up and cracking, as I'm trying to push through the reading of these gut-wrenching labels. Labels placed up there on that blank slate by people just like you and just like me. Labels that have been put upon us, the children of God—children who do not deserve to carry the pain and burden of such awful, God-forsaken labels. And I weep as I read...

UGLY
NOT GOOD ENOUGH
BROKEN
INCAPABLE
SLUT
UNWORTHY
UNLOVABLE
STUPID
NOT WORTH IT
UNWANTED
LESS THAN
INCOMPETENT

UNDESERVING
UNGRATEFUL
CRAZY
BAD
DEFECTIVE
LAZY
DISGUSTING

And the list of labels goes on and on, until I feel like my heart is about to break into pieces inside my chest. Beautiful people believing such ugly lies. Lies that impact them and influence the way they live. Lies that they were never intended to believe. Labels that they were never required to hold on to. I ask you this: What would your label say?

The God Who Comes to Obliterate

Jesus came to begin something new. If our blank slate is filled with false labels, our God doesn't just come to add a few additional nice labels to the board. He doesn't just come to scribble *pretty* next to our *ugly* labels—He comes to completely obliterate the old labels. He comes to give us a brand-new identity by wiping the entire slate away— every single one of those awful words—and starting from scratch, beginning all over again. The apostle Paul reminds us, "Anyone who belongs to Christ has become a new person. The old life is gone; a new life has begun!" (2 Corinthians 5:17 NLT). The old is dead and gone. It's time for something new. Starting from scratch with our identity can be a difficult process, especially when we've believed lies about ourselves for so long. That's why this process cannot be accomplished outside of God's Word.

Years ago, long before I met my husband, John, I went through a difficult breakup that I share about in my book *True Love Dates*.[3] I had wrapped up so much of my identity in trying to find the right person that, after the relationship was over, I felt like I had lost myself. I didn't really know who I *was* standing alone. I had to face my tabula rasa, look my slate in the eye, and begin asking God to help me rip off all the false labels I had believed over the years. It was time for something new. I spent a lot of time unpacking who I was during that season of my life, which, looking back, was actually God's preparation for the next season in which I would meet the man I would marry. God knew that if I wanted to have a better understanding of the kind of man who would fit into my life, I had to have my identity secure.

God's Word was such a crucial part in the process of beginning to download the truth of who I was standing alone. Because when you get in God's Word, God's Word begins to get in you. Slowly, but surely, my eyes began to open to the reality of who I was in Christ, and what it meant for me to live out of truth. I can say with confidence that this time in my life was another layer of healing that God was bringing to my spirit and soul, moving me closer to becoming healthy and whole. Healing happens in layers. We can't heal everything all at once because it would be overwhelming. But, in time, God begins to help us peel back one layer at a time. This was the season that God was longing to bring healing into my beliefs about myself. But in order to heal from those beliefs, I had to come face-to-face with them.

> Healing happens in layers.

I knew that the one and only thing I could look to for a solid understanding of my identity was what God was saying about me. Because His words never change. His view of me is always the same—no matter what I do or don't do. No matter what I've accomplished or not accomplished. No matter what my relationship status or lack thereof. No matter what has been done to me or what I have done to others. He sees me through the lens of truth, and that's exactly how I needed to begin seeing myself. I opened His Word and began to download His truth into my mind and allow it to make its way into my spirit. God's Word spoke over my tabula rasa and told me exactly what I needed to hear:

- *That I have a purpose:* "You are the ones chosen by God, chosen for the high calling" (1 Peter 2:9 MSG).

- *That I am accepted:* "You are...to tell others of the...differ-ence he made for you—from nothing to something, from rejected to accepted" (1 Peter 2:9-10 MSG).

- *That I am noticed:* "You have searched me, LORD, and you know me" (Psalm 139).

- *That I am forgiven:* "He has taken [your sin] away, nailing it to the cross" (Colossians 2:14).

- *That I am loved:* "What great love the Father has lavished on us" (1 John 3:1).

These are the labels I needed to place over my life and heart. These are the things I needed to begin believing about myself. These are the truths that I needed to begin believing to counteract the lies.

I don't know what labels you have been carrying over the years, but I do know that God's Word can speak truth and love onto those labels—no matter how awful or real they may feel. Though we can't change our past experiences, we can change what we allow ourselves to believe as a result of those experiences. This is where we can take back power and control over the false things that have been spoken over us, or maybe even the false things we end up speaking over ourselves.

God's Word is full of truths about who we are in Christ and what it means to be a child of God. Maybe that's where some of you need to start—by taking inventory of whether or not you would even consider yourself a child of God. You can't work on your identity in Christ until you've allowed yourself to be in relationship with Christ. The invitation is there, and it's for all. If that's you, I want you to stop right here and flip to the very last page of this chapter. I want to make sure we pause so that I can talk you through a prayer—a prayer that will affirm your desire to enter a relationship with Jesus, starting the pro-cess of transforming the old into something new. God's Word tells us that it's no good to gain the whole world if we end up losing our soul in the end (Matthew 16:26). A book about health falls short unless we've acknowledged our need for spiritual health and received the gift of new life in Christ.

For those of us who are currently walking with Jesus, we must be intentional about regularly replacing the lies with truth. It's not a once and done process; we're constantly being bombarded with lies—lies that can quietly begin to make their home in our hearts if we're not evicting them with truth. Because human experiences are so different and unique, each of us needs to find the truth that speaks over our unique lies. Let's look at some of God's truth found in Scripture. Ask yourself which of these truths you need to use to counteract the labels and lies you have believed:

- I am complete (Colossians 2:10).
- I am capable through Christ (Philippians 4:13).
- I am taken care of (Philippians 4:19).
- I am free (Romans 8:2).
- I am redeemed (Ephesians 1:7).
- I am wonderfully made (Psalm 139:14).
- I am precious (Isaiah 43:4).
- I am created in the image of God (Genesis 1:27).
- I am protected (Deuteronomy 31:6).

I challenge you to dig into God's Word and come face-to-face with what you believe about yourself—and whether or not it lines up with truth. We need to become people who believe truth over lies because what we believe about ourselves determines the level of our spiritual health. And what we believe about ourselves determines the kind of life we live.

Hello, my name is _____. The way you fill in that blank has the power to change your life.

Pray with Me

Jesus, I thank You that You love me enough to open my eyes to truth. I recognize that I can't fully know who I am until I know You. Today, I affirm that I want to be in relationship with You. I believe that You've died on the cross to take away my sins, I believe that You rose from the dead to make a way for me to be with You for eternity. I want to live for You today and always. I want to see myself through Your eyes. Fill me with Your Spirit and give me the grace I need to live for You each day. In the name of Jesus, amen.

If you prayed this prayer for the first time in your life, I want you to know that I am overjoyed! In fact, I want to hear from you. Email me at debra@truelovedates.com, and let me help you take the next steps on your journey with Jesus.

Journaling Questions: 5-Minute Spiritual Checkup

- Why is my view of myself important to my spiritual health?

- Are there any "black and blue buttons" or "emotional bruises" that tend to come out in my interactions with others?

- What are some of the false labels that have been placed on me over the years?

- What is one specific false label that I tend to struggle with believing?

- What does God's Word speak over my false label? Make a list of Scripture verses to speak truth over each false label.

- *Hello, my name is* _____. How would I fill in that blank in this season of my life?

6

Significant Others

My View of Relationships

The phrase "significant other" has always bothered me.

It's become part of the cultural lingo, and when it's spoken, we all understand that we're talking about someone that's more than just a friend—someone who carries a significant place of value and priority in someone's life. A boyfriend or a girlfriend, a fiancé, or a spouse. It's a term that implies love, romance, and physical attraction. It's a term that reminds us that we hold someone just as significantly as they hold us.

But I wonder if our simple acceptance of the phrase reflects something inherently wrong with our cultural view of relationships. Western society bases value and worth within the status of our romantic relationships. We are told that we are only valuable when we've found someone to tell us so. We're taught that we're only complete when we've found romantic love. And not only that, but we live in a culture that caters to this mentality. It's plastered on our television screens and commercials, our billboards and our magazines. It's blatant in our movies, our music, and our literature.

But what if, with our blind acceptance of the terminology, we've also accepted the lie that the most significant relationships in our lives are the ones that include physical attraction, sexual chemistry, and romantic experiences. What if we've started to believe that we're most significant when we find someone who we can call our own? We spend our lives in pursuit of this "one" relationship, all while neglecting the reality that maybe, just maybe, significance can be found in so many other places.

> We spend our lives in pursuit of this "one" relationship, all while neglecting the reality that maybe, just maybe, significance can be found in so many other places.

As much as I see beauty within the context of a romantic relationship and as much as I've been overwhelmingly blessed within the committed relationship of my marriage, there is a deep part of me that revolts against the mentality that our most significant relationships can only take shape within the framework of a romantic relationship. In fact, it's not biblical. As meaningful as my marriage is and as much as I am in love with my husband, my marriage is not—no, it *cannot*—be the only relationship that holds "significance" in my life.

Each and every stage of my life has ushered me into significant relationships, ordained by God to shape me, guide me, and make me into the person that I am today. From my respect and love of my parents for how they've shaped me, to my deep adoration of my children and how they challenge me; from my valuable interactions with my best friends who sharpen me, to the way that my mentors pour their lives into mine...there have been so many relationships in my life that have been of complete and utter significance.

Each significant relationship is ordained by God for a specific time, a specific place, and for the very specific purpose of making us more like Jesus. Each significant relationship brings us one step closer to our destiny, our calling, and the person God invites us to become.

But have we gotten so lost in the pursuit of a significant other that we've failed to realize the significance that's all around us? How many times in our myopic vision of relationships, in our obsession with romance, have we failed to see the bigger picture?

Love Is the Gauge

All throughout Scripture, we're encouraged to invest in significant relationships within the body of believers. We're called to intimate community and to meaningful fellowship. In fact, it's in community that we begin to get a gauge of our own spiritual health. Scripture goes so far as to say that how we love (or don't love) others is indicative of how much we love God: "Whoever claims to love God yet hates a brother or sister is a liar. For whoever does not love their brother and sister, whom they have seen, cannot love God, whom they have not seen" (1 John 4:20). Not only that, but the greatest command in all of Scripture comes down to two things: the way we love God and the way we love others (Matthew 22:37-39). It's safe to say, then, that one of the best measures we can have of our spiritual health is found in taking inventory of how well we love others. First John 4:7-12 words it so well:

> Dear friends, let us love one another, for love comes from God. Everyone who loves has been born of God and knows God. Whoever does not love does not know God, because God is love. This is how God showed his love among us: He sent his one and only Son into the world that we might live through him.
>
> This is love: not that we loved God, but that he loved us and sent his Son as an atoning sacrifice for our sins. Dear friends, since God so loved us, we also ought to love one another. No one has ever seen God; but if we love one another, God lives in us and his love is made complete in us.

When we love others, we're saying (without words) that we've actually glimpsed God's love for us (1 John 4:19). We're saying that we've been touched by His love, and it's impacting the way we love others.

If that's what Scripture tells us, then the opposite is also true. When we aren't loving others well, we're proving that we haven't really grasped God's love. We're not there yet because we just don't get God's love enough, or it would impact the way we love others.

> It's in community that we begin to get a gauge of our own spiritual health.

Love is the gauge, and as hard as it might be for us to admit, the way we love others is a huge indicator of how spiritually healthy we really are. Not only that, but the way we allow ourselves to be loved by others can be an avenue that brings healing and hope into our lives.

Healing Relationships

For many people, healing from harmful relationships comes from engaging in the opposite: healthy relationships. The ultimate source of healing, of course, is Jesus. By His wounds, we are healed, and through His sacrifice, we have the hope of eternity (Isaiah 53:5). Yet Jesus, by His grace and goodness, has allowed us to find earthly healing in the form of healthy earthly relationships. James 5:16 reminds us to "confess your sins to each another and pray for each other *so that you may be healed*" (emphasis added). Relationships are powerful, and they can be used to wound us or to heal us. They can be used to bring death or to bring life.

One of the most powerful stories I've ever heard depicting how this plays out comes from Wess Stafford, president emeritus of Compassion International. Born and raised as a missionary kid on the Ivory Coast, he found himself in a boarding school where he experienced terrible spiritual, sexual, and physical abuse at the hands of those in charge. "We were beaten regularly," he said in an interview. "There were a million reasons to get a beating—as simple as a wrinkle in your bed spread...seventeen times a week, sometimes to the place where you couldn't walk. I screamed into my pillow for mercy."[1] But, over a series of difficult events, Wess went on to explain that one day something switched in his brain, and he decided to finally stand up to the abuse: "I went from victim to victor. I had finally taken a stand...I knew at that point that this is what I do: I fight for children. I am the one who speaks up for children, for those who can't speak up for themselves."

At the young age of ten, Wess Stafford knew that the same relationships that had caused his pain would be the very relationships that would fuel his passion—his passion for speaking up for hurting children, which has led to the rescuing of over a million children from poverty through the ministry of Compassion International. He has found healing from his past through the healthy relationships he was able to foster in the present, by helping children from all around the world, shaping his pain into his purpose. What a beautiful picture of the healing power of healthy relationships!

> God can use healthy relationships in our present to bring healing from harmful relationships in our past.

Three People You Need in Your Life

Throughout Scripture, we're given many examples of healing relationships—people God used to bring healing and hope into the lives of the hurting. Some come in the form of the people we serve and disciple, like Wess Stafford, others come in the form of the people who pour into and disciple us, and still others come in the form of the people who walk by our side and sharpen us on the journey of life. Let's take some time to walk through three healing relationships and how we see them play out in Scripture.

Mentor: A Barnabas

Paul is considered to be one of the greatest teachers and preachers

of early Christianity. When we think of Paul, we think of the preaching of the gospel with power and passion. But he didn't get there alone.
In fact, Paul initially began his journey as a Christian with the help of
a man named Barnabas. After Paul (known at the time as Saul), had
a radical encounter with Jesus on the road to Damascus (Acts 9), the
majority of believers were afraid to interact with him. How could they
trust that this man who used to radically persecute Christians was now
preaching the gospel and safe to be around? But it was Barnabas who
took Paul under his wing, testified on his behalf, and paved the way for
Paul to connect with the disciples in Jerusalem (Acts 9:27).

Later, in Acts 11, we see that Paul was summoned by Barnabas to
come and help him minister to a new church planted in the city of
Antioch. For one year, Paul worked with Barnabas, assisting him as he
discipled a group of new believers. Barnabas, who was older and spiritually mature, invested in Paul during that time in his life. He mentored him and poured into him so that Paul could continue pouring
out to others. Here we see a beautiful example of the idea of mentorship as it's represented in Scripture.

Every single believer should have a mentor in their life. Someone
who is pouring into them, investing in them, and guiding them along
the path of faith. Someone who has gone ahead of them, experienced
things they haven't yet, and can give guidance and perspective along
the journey of life. When it comes to finding someone who would be
a good mentor, think of someone who is ten to twenty years ahead of
you—someone whom you look up to in their life, their faith, and their
relationships, whose life you look at and think, *That's where I want to
be one day.* And then, invite them into your life.

Sometimes mentorship relationships happen naturally, but most
often *you* have to be deliberate about inviting someone into your life
and asking them to be your mentor. I have had a mentor in every season of my life. In college, there was a psychology professor I really
looked up to. One day, in the ladies' bathroom in the science hall,
I walked in to find her washing her hands. It's a little awkward to

chitchat with toilets flushing in the background, but I knew this was my chance. I approached her right there and asked her if she would be willing to mentor me. What a gift it was to be under her wisdom for the remaining years of my time as a college student. She poured so much wisdom into my life, prayed over me, and encouraged me at a time when I needed it the most.

Fast-forward a few years. After getting married, a few moves, and a new baby. I needed some company and support, so I joined a mom's group. That's where I first met Brenda. She was the first face I saw as I walked in the door, and her infectious warmth made her stand out to me immediately. She was one of the leaders of the group, and her love for Jesus was evident in everything she did. I knew I would benefit so much from having her in my life, so a few months into getting to know her, I asked her to be my mentor. Brenda has been walking alongside of me through the joys and struggles of my life. She's watched me develop into an author, prayed over me for every speaking engagement, visited me when I was feeling sick, walked me through bouts of depression and anxiety, and celebrated with me in my victories. She's given me marriage and parenting advice, pointed me to Jesus, and taught me so many lessons through the experiences of her own life. I have benefited so much from sitting under her wisdom and love. And my spiritual health has been bolstered as a result of having her in my life. She pours into me so that I can pour into others.

Who is pouring into you? Who are the people you have "set yourself under" so that you can benefit from the wisdom and faith that is pouring out of them? A mentor relationship is a healing relationship, and one that each one of us should be deliberate about engaging in.

Friend: A Silas

"As iron sharpens iron, so one person sharpens another" (Proverbs 27:17). If we continue watching the life of Paul, we find that later on in his ministry he was joined by a man named Silas, the brother from another mother. Paul and Silas partnered together in ministry.

They had different personalities and different giftings, but they worked together to make Jesus known, and eventually, they were put in prison as a result. But they encouraged one another in the faith by praying together and singing praises to the Lord even while they were in prison (Acts 16:25). This is the kind of healing relationship I think about when I hear the scripture about iron sharpening iron. Iron is a strong metal standing alone. But in order to sharpen a piece of iron and make it more effective, you need to use another piece of iron. Silas was Paul's iron. They sharpened each other and pushed each other toward Jesus.

The same goes for each one of us as Christians. We need someone in our life who is sharpening us. Someone with a similar strength and commitment to Jesus, who can pray for us and sing praises with us when we're in a place of hardship. Someone who will always point us back to Jesus.

John and I have moved around a whole lot over the years as a result of his journey toward becoming a doctor. We lived in Illinois while he finished medical school, and then we moved to Pennsylvania during his residency training. Moving around can be difficult because each time we made new friends, we then had to uproot. After medical school, John got assigned to a fellowship (specialized training) in Florida. It was a one-year training, and the good news is that we would live by the beach for one year. But the bad news is that we would have to uproot our family yet again. We had developed such a strong, close-knit community in Pennsylvania, and thinking of leaving such great friends was a very difficult thing. Personally, friendships are extremely important to me, and thinking of losing my "sharpening friends" brought an ache to my heart. But God was asking us to trust Him.

When we moved to Florida, I was introduced to the wife of another one of the fellows John was working with. Her name was Erin. We had the same number of children, and our husbands worked at the same place. So, naturally, we became friends. But here's where the story gets good. Erin and her husband, Justin, were not only spending the year in Florida like us, but they were also solid believers. They loved

Jesus with all of their hearts, and our families soon became the best of friends. Over the course of that year, Erin became my "iron sharpens iron" friend. God's people were everywhere. I just had to look for them!

After that year in Florida, wouldn't you know it, God had both of our families find jobs in Pennsylvania, and we now live only 20 minutes apart. Erin is truly one of my best friends. More than that, she's like a sister to me. She checks in with me daily, prays over me routinely, and has walked by my side through thick and thin over the past six years. Her faith and love for the Lord have brought so much perspective into my heart as I've watched her walk through her own hardships, clinging to Jesus the whole way through. I'm so grateful for "iron sharpens iron" friends, and I see why God's Word is so clear about these healing relationships.

> God's people were everywhere. I just had to look for them!

The friends you are surrounded by have the power to bring life and death. They have the power to build you up or tear you down. Bad company corrupts good character, and your life is being shaped and sharpened by the people you allow into your life (1 Corinthians 15:33). In fact, it's commonly said that you will become like the five friends you're closest to. What a sobering reminder to be deliberate about the friends we're walking beside. It's a reminder that finding good friends should not be a passive pursuit, but an active one. Who are you allowing to come alongside you as you are walking the journey of life? Are they people who are pointing you to Jesus, or people who are keeping you from Him? Who is your Silas?

Disciple: A Timothy

Paul was deliberate about the people he surrounded himself with. One of those people was a young man by the name of Timothy (Acts 16). Timothy was a young believer with so much potential, and Paul was adamant about taking him along on the journey to teach him and train him in the faith. So, young Timothy joined Paul and learned from him along the way.

Paul was intentional about pouring into Timothy. That is the beauty found in the healing relationship of discipleship. It's a relationship that allows us to pour out freely all that God has given to us. Unlike an "iron sharpens iron" friendship, a discipleship relationship is a relationship in which we give and pour out with no expectation of receiving anything in return. Your legacy will only go as far as the people you disciple because those are the people who carry what you've given them into the next generation. Jesus so willingly and intentionally poured into His 12 disciples, and that pouring out—eventually the pouring out of His very life—became the catalyst that changed the entire world.

Discipleship has looked different in different seasons of my life. When I was young and single, I had a lot more free time than I do today, and it seemed easier to invest in discipleship relationships. I was in charge of an inner-city ministry for at-risk youth, and it wasn't uncommon to see me driving a big SUV full of kids that I was mentoring and discipling. Pouring into them was so life-giving for me. It filled me with purpose and joy! So, I can clearly see why this type of relationship can be so healing.

These days, my primary disciples are my children: Elisabeth, Elijah, and Ezra. (And yes, they all have biblical names that begin with *E*. I always say that it might get tricky if we decide to have any more children because finding more biblical *E* names that you like starts to get difficult after three. I mean, sure, we could go with Eldad, Ecclesiastes, or Ephesians, but like I said...it gets tricky.) On the one hand, I look at my children and see what a huge responsibility and honor it is to have the chance to disciple these little people—to pour into them and point them to Jesus. I'm so grateful for the privilege to do so, and I take it seriously. In fact, I've committed my entire life to this cause, which is the primary reason our family has chosen the avenue of homeschooling.

But on the other hand, I want my children to watch me disciple others as well. I want them to see me serve, love, disciple, and pour into others. I want them to see that being a mom is not the only role God has called me to, and that being their mom is not the only healing relationship in my life. Because what they see is ultimately what they will model. So, with the little free time I do have, I try to be deliberate. Each season of my life, I make room for one—just one—young woman that I feel God has called me to come alongside. Sometimes, she comes over to the house while I'm schooling, and then we sit and chat over a cup of coffee while my kids have their free time. Other times, it's FaceTime, phone calls, texts, and emails. But no matter what shape discipleship takes in different seasons of my life, I want to do my part in giving as I have been given, in helping as I have been helped, in mentoring as I have been mentored.

Maybe you're reading this and thinking, "Well, you're a mom," or "You're a counselor," or "You've been a Christian for so many years." Maybe you're reading this feeling like you have nothing to offer, nothing to pour out. I want to stop you right here and affirm that no matter who you are or what you've come from, you have a role in giving to others. You have something someone else needs. Maybe it's your past experiences. Maybe it's in the lessons you've learned from the mistakes you've made. Maybe it's your listening ear. Maybe it's your loving heart. Maybe it's simply your kind eyes. You have something that someone needs, and God wants to use you to bless as you have been blessed. How are you being deliberate about inviting the healing relationship of discipleship into your life?

The Spiritual Health of the Body

As I mentioned in the beginning of this chapter, how we love is the gauge of how healthy we are spiritually. God's Word reminds us that, as Christians, we're all represented as different body parts but part of one body. In order to know whether the body is healthy, we have to see if it's growing. How does the body of Christ grow? We find our answer in Ephesians 4:15-16 (emphasis added):

> Speaking the truth in *love*, we will grow to become in every respect the mature body of him who is the head, that is, Christ. From him the whole body, joined and held together by every supporting ligament, grows and builds itself up in *love*, as each part does its work.

Love. Not only is our personal spiritual health evidenced by how we love, but also the health of the body of believers—the church. As the body of Christ, we can only grow when we're building one another up in love, where each one of us is taking seriously our individual role to love one another and give to one another and invest in healing relationships. Our entire spiritual identity is linked to this one thing, Jesus says, "By this everyone will know that you are my disciples, if you love one another" (John 13:35). Our entire calling is love: "Let no debt remain outstanding, except the continuing debt to love one another, for whoever loves others has fulfilled the law" (Romans 13:8). Love. This is the message we heard from the very beginning and one that continues today (1 John 3:11).

I often look around at all that's going on in the body of Christ—from dissent in political opinions to disagreement in theological interpretation to the heart-wrenching poverty and persecution that the church is facing in many parts of the world. And I find myself wondering, *How healthy is the body of Christ?*

It's easy to paint the church with the broad brushstroke of judgment, seeing its flaws and failures as an entire body. But what's harder—and, dare I say, more productive—is when we can begin to look at the health of each individual body part and take inventory of the health of the only part of the body we are responsible for: ourselves. How have I contributed to the health—or lack thereof—of the body of Christ? How have I engaged in Christian community with my brothers and sisters in Christ, and have I added to the growth of the body by how I love, or weakened the body with my lack of love?

> How have I contributed to the health—or lack thereof—of the body of Christ?

What would someone say about the

health of your individual body part if they took inventory of your conversations, your conflict management, or your emotional temperament in how you deal with people? What would someone say about the health of your personal body part if they scrolled through your comments and interactions on social media, peeked through your email exchanges, or swiped through your Internet history? How are you reflecting love to the people around you? How is your spiritual health impacting the growth—or lack thereof—of the body of Christ?

The Context of Community: Your Social Map

It's hard to see your personal shortcomings when you're standing alone. Because when you're alone, it's easy to be kind, gracious, and loving toward yourself. It's easy to forgive your sins, have grace with your mistakes, and cover your wrongdoings—a whole lot easier than it is to do those things for others, anyway. In fact, Jesus reminds us how easy it is to see the flaws of others, all the while overlooking our own (Matthew 7:5).

But in the context of community, we're forced to come face-to-face with what we bring to the table of relationships. In the context of community, we emotionally and spiritually rub up against people in ways that bring out both the best and the worst in us. Community can be a great opportunity for healing because it invites us to take ownership of our portion of the relationship equation. But we can only make the most of community if we're engaging in community.

> We can only make the most of community if we're engaging in community.

Sometimes, it's easier to avoid the mess of relationships by not engaging in relationships at all. Maybe we don't do this purposely; oftentimes, it happens unconsciously. To try to avoid the hurt, pain, and effort of relationships, sometimes it's easier to isolate. I worked with a young man who had a tendency to avoid relationships. Whenever I prompted him to share about the people closest to him, he would always get flustered, and then his list would fall short. "I guess I don't really let people in," he concluded one day, "I guess it's just easier to keep them out."

Here's my question to you: Are you letting people into your life? If love is the gauge of spiritual health, and we can only love those who we're in relationship with, then it would follow that stream of thinking to start by taking inventory of the people we've allowed into our life. Our community is the catalyst for our love. Take a minute right now to do a little activity taking inventory of your social map. Think about the people who are closest to you—the people you have allowed into your life—and then map them in your journal using the graph below.

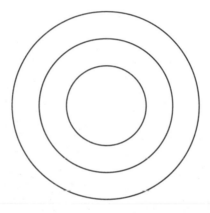

The first and smallest circle is what I'll call the inner circle or your core group. These are the people who are closest to you in your life. They're the people that know it all: the good, the bad, and the ugly. They're the ones you go to when you need support or simply want to celebrate. In these relationships, you hold nothing back. Jot down a few names of people who are in your inner circle.

The second circle of people are what we'll call your friends. They're people that you invest in and interact with on a regular basis, but you've never fully let them in. They may know a lot about you, but they certainly don't know everything. They're people that you respect and appreciate, but they're not the people who are closest to your heart. Write down some names of friends in circle two.

The third and outer circle represents your acquaintances. These are people who you may interact with casually but not intentionally. They may be coworkers, friends at church, or distant family members. But overall, they're people you interact with by default, meaning they are familiar people who happen to be present in places you frequent, but they're not relationships that you're being intentional about.

Now, let's analyze your social map a bit, shall we? What can we learn about you by looking at this map? First of all, ask yourself this: Are there too many people on the map or too few? Too many people tells me that your focus is on the quantity of the relationships but not necessarily on the quality of the relationships. Too few people tells me that there may be some things that are holding you back in fully investing in relationships: trust issues, fear, or even apathy.

Which circle has the greatest number of people? If it's circle one, you should ask yourself if you're spreading yourself too thin in your closest relationships by trying to be a person who pleases everyone. As human beings, we all have a maximum amount of emotional energy to invest, and we have to make sure we're not spreading ourselves too thin in relationships. Is circle three the largest group? That could indicate that your comfort zone is with superficial relationships—interactions that don't get too messy because you never get too close. If level two is the largest group, that could mean you're very intentional about who you let in your life versus who you don't let in.

If spiritual health happens in the context of community, then being deliberate about the community you surround yourself with is an important aspect of moving toward spiritual health. What might be holding you back, and how can you begin to be more intentional with the people God has placed in your life?

Love's Got Everything to Do with It

"What's love got to do with it?" Tina Turner asked in her 1993 hit song. *Everything* is the answer. Love has got everything to do with it.

Community plays a huge role in our spiritual health. Are our significant relationships filled with conflict and drama? Do we allow people to get close to us, or do we keep them at a distance? Do we find ourselves engaging in give-and-take relationships, or do we get stuck with one-sided relationships? How we engage with the world and in community is revealing.

It's time to recognize the many "significant others" God has surrounded us with and then invest in the people He's called us to. People who will encourage us, build us up, and call us out when we need to be corrected. People that He will use to shape us, challenge us, and help us grow. People who will be used by God to give us a glimpse of our own spiritual health, reminding us that love—and love alone—is the gauge.

Journaling Questions: 5-Minute Spiritual Checkup

- What do I typically think when I hear the phrase "significant other"?

- If how I love is the gauge of my spiritual health, what can I do to work on loving better? Is there any relationship in which I need to show more love?

- When it comes to healing relationships, who are the people I've invited into my life (or could invite) in the following categories?
    - Mentor _____
    - Friend _____
    - Disciple _____

- What did I learn about myself during the social map activity? What's a way I can be more intentional about the community I've allowed into my life?

PART 3

Mental Health
Getting Real with Your Mind

Love the Lord your God...with all your mind.
LUKE 10:27

7

What's on Repeat?

Cognitive Distortions

Did you know that you can change the shape and function of your brain?

It's true. Your brain is malleable, like a piece of dough, shaped by thoughts and experiences. The scientific word for this is *plasticity* or *neuroplasticity*. Scientists used to believe that the brain could only be shaped during the earliest stages of development—in childhood and infancy. But the latest research understands that the human brain is much more malleable than we originally thought. It can be shaped anytime, anywhere, in anyone.[1] As writers Catherine Pittman and Elizabeth Karle put it,

> The circuits of your brain aren't determined completely by genetics; they're also shaped by your experiences and the way you think and behave. You can remodel your brain to respond differently, no matter what your age. There are

limits, but there's also a surprising level of flexibility and potential for change in your brain.[2]

This is fantastic news because it gives us the power to influence and impact our mental health. It means that we can truly be intentional with honoring God with our mind because we're not simply victims to our genetic wiring.

Thoughts → Feelings → Behaviors

The earliest psychologists believed that negative feelings led to negative thoughts. But over the years, psychologists have determined that it's actually the other way around. What we *think* actually triggers how we *feel*, which then impacts how we *behave*. But most people go about their day mindless to how their thoughts are actually impacting them, and unaware that they have the power to change those thoughts. Counselors and psychologists call the concept of taking ownership of your thoughts "cognitive behavioral therapy," but it was initially created by the best counselor around...God.

In Scripture, we see the principle of the power of changing your thoughts referred to as renewing your mind: "Do not conform to the pattern of this world, but be transformed by the renewing of your mind. Then you will be able to test and approve what God's will is—his good, pleasing and perfect will" (Romans 12:2). Whether we call it cognitive behavioral therapy or the renewing of our mind, the bottom line is this: Thought change leads to life change.

> Thought change leads to life change.

Illusions

I'm fascinated by optical illusions. When I was growing up, 3D pictures were all the rage. They were called Magic Eye pictures. If you don't know what I'm talking about, please do me a favor and stop what you're doing and go Google them. They're amazing. Basically, a Magic Eye photo was a patterned image of different shapes and colors, but what you saw superficially wasn't the image you were supposed to see. There was always a picture hidden within the picture, and the only way you could see the secret picture was by looking "past" the picture, allowing your eyes to blur, and then all of a sudden, another image would emerge. I used to say when I grew up I was going to have Magic Eye pictures all over my home, but now that décor style seems rather '90s.

What is most incredible to me is the idea that what we see superficially isn't always what's there. Oftentimes, what we see superficially is just an illusion. Usually, there's more to the story if we take the time to stop, be intentional, and see the big picture. The same goes for our thought life. Whether or not you're aware of this, you have a default pattern of thinking. It's your superficial cognitive response to your experiences. Another way of wording this would be to call them your "automatic thoughts." We all have automatic thoughts— things we think without a conscious decision to think those things. The thing we have to be most aware of about our automatic thoughts is that sometimes we're not really seeing the big picture. Sometimes what we're thinking isn't accurate or complete. Sometimes we find ourselves thinking thoughts because it's the easiest way to think. It's the way we've always thought. It's easy and superficial and doesn't take too much work.

When it comes to our thought process, our brain loves the path of least resistance. *What I've done most often is the easiest thing to do again because it takes the least amount of work.* Thoughts included. The problem with that response is that too often our default patterns of thinking are unhealthy and often untrue. But we can't change what we don't recognize.

The Brain Scam

Scammers have become all too common in our country today, and with the rise of technology, we've also seen a rise in scams. Often, scams come in the form of a phone call, an email, or a letter that seems so accurate—so close to reality that it tempts you to believe it's true, when it's actually not. As a writer and blogger, I'm on my computer a decent amount, so I'm always privy to the latest scam. One day, I was in the middle of writing with a deadline looming around the corner. All of a sudden, I saw a message that took over my entire screen telling me that my computer had a massive virus and that all my data would be lost unless I called the phone number on my screen and gave them information that would allow them to shut down the virus and save my data. Thankfully, this isn't the first time something like this has happened to me, so I knew to simply "x" out the screen, ignore it, and continue working as usual. But years ago, I wasn't so informed. The first time this scam ever happened to me, I frantically shut down my computer in a panic and called John. He did a quick Google search, found out the warning message on my computer was a scam, and told me not to worry about it. But not everyone reacts that way. In fact, many people call the number and end up giving scammers important personal information such as social security numbers and credit card numbers out of a lack of awareness. They don't recognize it's a scam, so they give in to it and end up being victims of identity theft.

The brain can *fool* us into believing something that's not actually true. We can be victims to the brain scam. The default patterns of thinking that I mentioned above can be used by our brain to trick us into seeing life in a way that's not accurate or healthy. In counseling and psychology, we call this concept *cognitive distortions*.

Cognitive distortions are essentially distorted or inaccurate ways of thinking. Not only do we all have some cognitive distortions, but for some of us, they're our primary way of thinking. They're on repeat in our brain, like a song that gets stuck in our head. In order to take responsibility for our thoughts, we have to first recognize the cognitive distortions that we're dealing with and begin to replace them with truth.

In counseling, we call that cognitive restructuring. It's like taking that song that's stuck in our head and replacing it with a better song.

Before we get into how reframing and restructuring work, I want to clue you in to ten of the most common brain scams or cognitive distortions. As you read through this list, ask yourself which ones you tend to use most often, and reflect on how these cognitive distortions might be impacting the health of your thoughts, your emotions, and your behaviors.

Black-and-white thinking or all-or-nothing thinking. People who struggle with this cognitive distortion have a tendency to see things in extremes, rather than having a balanced perspective. They look at things as either black or white, good or bad, helpful or unhelpful, etc, without considering that there may be shades of gray. Things are either amazing, or they're terrible.

A practical example of this would be the mom who feels so overwhelmed that one day she impulsively decides to clear out everything on her calendar. She cancels her appointments and backs out of her commitments. Instead of seeing shades of gray by looking at some things she can prune from her schedule, she wipes it all out instead. It's either black, or it's white. It's either all, or it's nothing. This is a dangerous way of thinking because it can also impact how you feel about yourself. If you mess up, you're a failure. If you do well, you're wonderful. This extreme way of thinking often leads to intense emotions and impulsive reactions. Healthy people learn to think and process with balance.

Overgeneralization. This cognitive distortion is when you take one negative experience or interaction and generalize it to everything else. For example, your boss might comment on the fact that you didn't complete an assignment properly, and instead of seeing it as an isolated incident, you overgeneralize and assume that your boss must be disappointed with everything you're doing at work. It begins to impact your attitude at work and the way you interact with your boss thereafter. You take one negative experience, and you transfer it onto the entirety of your situation.

Minimization and magnification. This cognitive distortion happens when you have a tendency to make light of the good things and/or exaggerate the bad things. For example, someone might comment and say they love your outfit. Instead of being grateful for the compliment, you would minimize and say something like, "Oh, I got this old thing at a thrift store." Magnification, on the other hand, is when you exaggerate the negative. Your husband might tell you that he's not a big fan of that new shirt you got, and next thing you know, all you can think about is that comment and start to question what other things he must not love about you.

Mind reading. This distortion happens when we assume that we know what someone else is thinking, although we haven't confirmed it to be true. And typically, with mind reading, what we assume is something negative. I remember when I was in high school, and one of my best friends walked by me in the hallway, and I greeted her with a big smile and hello. She looked me right in the eyes, totally ignored me, and kept on walking. I was so hurt! *She must be really angry with me! What did I do to make her so upset?* My mind was buzzing with thoughts about that interaction all day, replaying our past conversations from the week. At the end of the day, she showed up at my car like usual for a ride home. "Hey! Ready to go?" she said with a smile. I was so confused. "What's the matter?" she said when she noticed the look on my face. When I explained to her about the incident in the hall, she had no idea what I was talking about. In fact, she hadn't even seen me like I assumed she did! She had just gotten out of a class where she had received a really bad test score, and she was stressing about what her parents might say. She didn't even see me waving at her in the hall because her mind was occupied with something else.

Mind reading is such a common cognitive distortion, and it has the power to ruin relationships when we assume rather than ask what's going on in someone else's mind. As a relationship counselor, I find that married couples struggle with this on a regular basis. Rather than ask, they assume what the other person is thinking, which ends up leading to false beliefs and hurt feelings in the end.

Fortune-telling. This distortion impacts the way you see the future. It's the assumption that something is going to turn out in a negative way, when you don't have evidence that it will because it hasn't happened yet! It's forecasting hardships before they've occurred. It could come in the form of thinking you're going to "fail that test," "not get the promotion," or "lose my friend." Maybe it comes in the form of the single man or woman who thinks, "I'm never going to find someone to spend the rest of my life with." Either way, it causes you to think negative thoughts about the future, convincing yourself that the worst-case scenario is just around the corner before anything has occurred.

Catastrophizing. This distortion lives up to its name because people who struggle with this way of thinking tend to make catastrophes out of everything. They're constantly thinking in worst-case scenarios. In other words, they make a mountain out of a molehill. Something legitimate can happen that's truly uncomfortable or difficult, but mentally it becomes exaggerated to the point that it's unbearable and impossible because their brain turns it into a possible catastrophe.

An example of this might be someone catching a cold or the flu, and then finding their thoughts fixating on all the other terrible things that might be physically wrong with them. Maybe they'll get online and search for the all terrible illnesses this could be, and ultimately convince themselves that they're likely going to die. The struggle becomes a catastrophe because of how it is being cognitively processed, and not because the struggle itself is insurmountable.

Emotional reasoning. This distortion is a common one because it allows our feelings to lead the way. The underlying assumption with this faulty way of thinking is this: Just because I feel it, it must be true. It allows our feelings to dictate our reality, instead of the other way around. An example of this would be the man who quits his job because he feels incompetent, even though no one has alluded that he's not doing a good job at his place of work. Emotional reasoning is when we follow feelings rather than facts. And like we mentioned in an earlier chapter, it's a dangerous way of thinking because our feelings aren't always accurate.

Should-could-would statements. This distortion puts your mental focus on the past, as you process and reprocess the things you should have done, could have done, or would have done if you could go back in time. The problem with this way of thinking is that it keeps you stuck. Rather than living in the present and hopeful for the future, you find yourself ruminating on the past and things that can't be changed.

I worked with a young man who lost his twin brother at a young age in a tragic accident. He spent so much of his thought life replaying the incident, wondering if he could have saved his brother if he had done things differently. His thoughts were so focused on the past that they impacted his ability to enjoy the present. Everything was tainted by traces of regret—things he should have done or could have done differently. This way of thinking is detrimental because it keeps us from healing and from moving forward.

Labeling. In chapter 5, we talked about the labels that we carry—words that have been placed on us by others or even by ourselves. This cognitive distortion comes down to the way we perceive ourselves or others. It's a word or judgment we place upon someone that influences our beliefs and interactions. Stereotyping is a great example of this cognitive distortion—assuming things about someone based on a label we give them.

Additionally, we might label someone as "ignorant" and then interact with them based on the belief we've formed that they're not intelligent or aware. We might label ourselves as "awkward" and then see ourselves through the lens of social incompetence every time we interact with someone. Labels are cognitive distortions that negatively impact our perception of others as well as our perception of ourselves.

Personalization. This distortion happens when we assume responsibility for things that do not belong to us. We take things personally and make them about us, rather than seeing them objectively. For example, you're hanging out with a friend who is acting rather irritable, and you automatically think she's upset with you. You take her mood personally by assuming it has something to do with you. This distortion can cause a lot of difficult feelings and wrong beliefs because every negative experience or interaction gets traced back to you.

What's on Repeat?

When my kids were younger, every time we would hop in the car, the automatic request was for me to play their "kids' songs" (who am I kidding—we're still in this stage). Gone were the days of listening to U2. So long, Elevation Worship. Now my mind would forever be filled with songs like "Arky Arky," "Give Me Oil in My Lamp," and "Father Abraham." One evening, I went out alone to finish an errand. I had the car to myself. But believe it or not, I drove around for about two hours until I realized that I had "Arky Arky" on repeat! I was so used to hearing it that it didn't even register that it was still playing in the background. I could have chosen *any other song on God's green earth*, but because I was so used to hearing it, I didn't think to change it.

Cognitive distortions are similar because they often happen so automatically and so often that we don't always recognize them. That's why I wanted to take the time to list them above. We'll do some additional work on recognizing cognitive distortions in our 5-Minute Checkup at the end of the chapter. Because the first step in freedom from negative patterns of thinking is to acknowledge them. And then after we've done that, the second step is to replace them.

Counselors call the act of replacing negative thoughts *cognitive restructuring*. What it means is changing your inaccurate thoughts and replacing them with healthier thoughts. It's not enough to recognize the distortion that's been on repeat in our mind. We have to take the next step of changing the song. This is why the process of counseling is an important step for those who find themselves battling cognitive distortions on a regular basis. It's crucial to have someone trained who can talk you through the distortions you're struggling with, how they may have been formed, and then suggest alternative, better ways of thinking. Because the thoughts that you hold impact the feelings you will have.

Which Side of the Story Are You Living In?

When it comes to how we see life, there are always two sides to the story you tell yourself. Two different lenses or interpretations by which we can see the world and what's happening in it. Let me give you an example.

The Dark Side

This past fall, John and I decided to take an adventurous family trip to Egypt. Since we're both Egyptian by descent, we thought it would be an incredible way to introduce our children to the culture of their heritage. But sometimes adventures come with adversity. First of all, taking three children (one who is a toddler and another who gets extremely motion sick) on a 12-hour airplane ride should be considered an Olympic event. It was an overnight trip, and saying we got one hour of sleep that night would be an overstatement. When we arrived in Cairo, the seven-hour time difference was enough to keep us feeling jet-lagged and miserable for the first two days of our time there.

Second of all, the culture shock of going from a first-world country to a second-world country was something no one can really prepare for. The city of Cairo is one of the busiest and dirtiest cities in the world. There are people (and trash and stray animals) everywhere! The traffic in Cairo is unlike anything you've ever witnessed. There are absolutely no rules, and trying to cross the street meant literally putting your life at risk every single time. One day, my three-year-old bolted out onto the road, and I quickly grabbed his hand, pulling him back just in time before he got struck by a car.

We had to be extremely cautious about what we ate because ingesting the wrong thing could have made us very sick during our time there. John ended up getting sick while we were there and spent 12 hours in bed. Not only that, but both of our boys got carsick nearly every time we went anywhere because the traffic was so chaotic. Adventures often come with adversity, and I can certainly say Egypt was a trip we won't ever forget.

The Bright Side

This past fall, John and I decided to take an adventurous family trip to Egypt. Since we're both Egyptian by descent, we thought it would be an incredible way to introduce our children to the culture of their heritage. And it was truly a trip of a lifetime! Taking three children (one who is a toddler and another who gets extremely motion sick) was risky, but we brought tons of snacks and activities to keep them busy during the 12-hour airplane ride. To our surprise, the motion sickness medicine we gave our son did the trick, and he was perfectly fine the entire flight! It was an overnight trip, and saying we got one hour of sleep that night would be an overstatement, but we got to watch movies, play games, and listen to audiobooks. Our tolerance level for long trips has increased! There's nothing we can't tackle now.

The culture shock of going from a first-world country to a second-world country was something no one can really prepare for. But we did our best to talk our children through what they might experience, and our preparations seemed to lessen the shock. The city of Cairo is one of the busiest and dirtiest cities in the world, but it's rich in culture. There are people everywhere! The traffic in Cairo is unlike anything you've ever witnessed, but we were careful to only cross the street when we had to and stuck to private transportation. My kids said it felt like playing a game of "Crossy Roads," and we all got a laugh out of it.

We had to be careful about what we ate because ingesting the wrong thing could have made us very sick during our time there, but the food we did enjoy was incredible! Thankfully, John was the only one who got sick once. We were all in good health and able to do everything on our list and more, including seeing the Great Pyramids, boating down the Nile River, visiting the Cairo Museum, and snorkeling in the Red Sea. Every day was packed with new experiences, and it felt magical and surreal all at the same time. Adventures often mean taking risks, but I can certainly say that this was a trip of a lifetime and one that we will never, ever forget.

The Story You Tell Yourself

Even though they seem drastically different, both stories above are true. No exaggeration and no tweaking facts. Because no matter what story you're telling, there is always going to be the good side and the bad side, the dark side and the bright side. Life hands each one of us a story that's filled with both hardships and victories. While we may have control of how some of the details of our story play out, oftentimes, there are elements we can't control. The one thing we do have control of, though, is which side of the story we tend to spotlight in our minds. We may not be in charge of the whole story, but we're in charge of the way we tell the story to ourselves.

> We may not be in charge of the whole story, but we're in charge of the way we tell the story to ourselves.

There is so much power in the story you tell yourself—the story you allow to repeat over and over in your mind—because the story you tell yourself is your cognitive response to a situation. Your story reflects your thoughts. Your thoughts impact your feelings. And your feelings motivate your behaviors.

Taking Inventory

When it comes to your life, what story are you telling yourself? How do you process the things that happened to you in the past, the things you're experiencing in the present, or the way you think about your future? Which side of your story do you tend to live in—the dark side or the bright side? The side that's tainted by cognitive distortions or the side that's filled with truth and hope? Because the story you tell yourself determines how you will live. What's on repeat in your mind will influence what's on repeat in your life. Taking inventory of your mental health begins by taking inventory of your thoughts and asking yourself this important question: What's on repeat?

Journaling Questions: 5-Minute Mental Health Checkup

- Look through the list of cognitive distortions and write out the ones that you tend to struggle with the most (acknowledge the cognitive distortion).

- Write down the specific cognitive distortions that you have under each category you listed. For example, under black-and-white thinking: "*I'm a bad person because I struggle with sin.*"

- Now, look at the list of cognitive distortions you wrote out, and ask God to reveal to you His truth about that specific thought (replace the cognitive distortion with truth). For example: "*I am a sinner in need of grace, but because of God's redemption I am not a bad person—I am a child of God.*"

- Write down one example of how your negative thoughts cause negative feelings.

- Write down one example of how your negative feelings cause negative behaviors.

- Make this activity a weekly process until you begin to see freedom from your patterns of cognitive distortions. Consider inviting the help of a professional counselor.

- Consider writing out your current life experience in two narratives: "the dark side" and "the bright side." Which side do you tend to spotlight and live out of most often?

8

Anxiety, Depression, and the Church

Mental Health Matters

My brain had been hijacked.

Hijacked by postpartum hormones, by stress, and by a chemical imbalance that I couldn't see from the outside looking in. But not only did I fail to see what was going on inside of me, so did many of the people I loved and trusted the most.

I remember calling up a friend during one of the darkest moments of my life, in the thick of anxiety and depression. I couldn't see past the dark cloud that was looming overhead. I needed someone to help me see what I couldn't see—to tell me that there was hope, to show me that this was not a result of anything I did, to remind me that this was not the end of the story. Her advice to me was to pray more and to trust God more. She gave me some verses from the Bible to meditate on and pray that day, but how can you meditate when you can hardly string two thoughts together? How can you pray when all you feel is emptiness inside?

Historically, the church at large has not had the greatest reputation when it comes to responding to mental illness. In her book *Madness: American Protestant Responses to Mental Health*, Dr. Heather Vacek takes time to explore how this subject has been misunderstood and mishandled by people of faith over the years.[1] Underlying the failure to properly address this subject is the false belief that mental health issues could be rooted in sin or a lack of faith. People who struggle with mental illness are often encouraged to trust God more, to pray more, or to read Scripture in order to receive healing.

The problem is, we often confuse mental health with spiritual health, but the two are not one and the same. If anything, mental health has more in common with physical health than it does with spiritual health because the body-mind connection is one that can't be denied by modern science. The brain is a vital organ of the body, and when the brain is sick, it impacts every other part of the body. Mental illness doesn't reflect a character issue. It reflects a chemistry issue. And anyone who tells you otherwise doesn't have a proper understanding of mental illness.

> We often confuse mental health with spiritual health, but the two are not one and the same.

When someone is diagnosed with cancer, we encourage them to see an oncologist and seek radiation and chemotherapy as a method of treatment. When someone is diagnosed with diabetes, we encourage them to visit an endocrinologist and pursue medical treatment such as insulin. After that, we encourage them to change their lifestyle and to take care of their physical health and their nutrition intake. But when it comes to mental health issues, such as anxiety, depression, bipolar disorder, or post-traumatic stress disorder, we often fail to give the same encouragement. Instead, we tell them to pray. To confess. To have more faith. I asked my friends on social media to tell about the response they've received from the church at large toward their struggles with mental illness. The comments that came in were heartbreaking. I wonder if any of these comments echo your own experience:

- Unfortunately, the response I've received is that people want to put a Bible verse Band-Aid on the problem so that (unconsciously) they don't have to deal with the reality of your situation, but they feel like they've "helped" by sharing a verse.

- I have shared with other Christians about my struggles with depression. Either they feel sorry for me, truly empathize, and even open up about their own emotional challenges or rebuke me due to my "lack of faith in God's healing power."

- They want to shut it down almost as fast as it was brought up and dismiss the fact that mental illnesses exist.

- I grew up in a culture that said you have to pray harder and have enough faith. I've been told that depression isn't real, and it's all attention seeking.

- I've been told that you cannot experience both depression and the fruit of the Spirit. That Christians must feel joy on a physical level; otherwise, they have to repent and "get back on the right path."

- I was hurt by hearing a preacher say that antidepressants are just one more way that people "poison" themselves.

> Mental illness doesn't reflect a character issue; it reflects a chemistry issue.

Why do we treat an illness of the brain so differently than the other organs of the body? When cancer strikes, we start Facebook pages, prayer lists, and support groups. We deliver meals, take turns running errands, and offer physical and emotional support. But when mental illness rears its ugly head, we rebuke it with false claims. Worse yet, we hide from it or invalidate it. We pretend that it doesn't exist, forcing those struggling with it to battle through it alone. But it is exactly in those dark and lonely places that mental illness loves to feed, grow, and attack. It thrives in isolation.

Facing the Darkness

There is no darker place than the pit of mental illness. It's a place of dreaded emotion and unrelenting despair. It saps you of your hope, robs you of your joy, and even steals your very desire to live. It's a dark cloud that perpetually looms overhead, giving no sign of relief, no sign of the sun that shines above it. After a while, you begin to forget that the sun even exists.

It has no favorites and attacks when you least expect it. It doesn't care if you're rich or poor, churched or unchurched, young or old. It's an illness that paralyzes your body, grieves your emotions, and breaks your spirit. It starts in the mind and then begins to quietly impact every other part of your life. It's a quiet illness because it comes with a blanket of shame. It's as though those who struggle with depression are somehow less than. Less holy. Less Christian. Less courageous. Less strong.

What a lie from the pit of hell! I believe that some of the strongest people are those who have faced the ugly monster of mental illness yet keep moving forward. It's time to stop throwing out Bible verses and offering prayers without providing practical help for those who are depressed. It's like praying for a starving man without feeding him. We as Christians need to start being the instruments of hope and healing for those who are struggling. Sometimes, all it takes is a listening ear, a hand to hold, a shoulder to cry on, or someone to talk to. Sometimes, all it takes is someone to lead them toward getting some help. But first and foremost, it starts by bringing this illness—an illness that loves and thrives in isolation and darkness—into the light. Because it's only in the light that we can be healed. This is exactly and precisely why we as the church need to be a place that's talking about mental illness, inviting it INTO THE LIGHT, more than anyone else out there. We need to be the safe place where people can come just as they are, having nothing to hide.

This is where we as Christians have failed when it comes to the way we approach mental illness. When we offer spiritual Band-Aids instead of practical support. Certainly, prayer and the reading of God's Word is crucial to our spiritual health during times of struggle. But addressing the spiritual component without addressing the mental component ends up causing more harm than good because it neglects the source of the problem and fails to offer a solution. Properly addressing mental illness requires a proper understanding of mental illness. This is where we must begin.

Mental Malfunction

What's Happening in My Brain?

One of the first steps to inviting mental illness into the light is understanding it. What is happening in the mind and body when someone is suffering from mental illness? Since there are so many different mental illnesses that impact the mind and body in so many different ways, I'm going to focus on breaking down the two most common for the purpose of simplicity: anxiety and depression.

We must start this conversation by understanding that the brain is made up of many pathways called neurons. Neurons are the messengers that send signals from one part of the body to another part of the body. "They reach out to other neurons to receive messages, which travel between neurons by means of a chemical process."[2] The messages that are passed from one neuron to another come in the form of chemicals called neurotransmitters. Some examples of the neurotransmitters are adrenaline, dopamine, and serotonin. These chemicals are responsible for transferring information from one neuron to another— information that ultimately impacts your mind and body, telling it how to think, feel, and react.

Every sensation you experience, from the sight of these
words on the page to the sounds of birds singing in your
yard is processed in your brain by neurons. The sensations you experience, such as light waves that enter your
eyes or vibrations in the air that impact your eardrums,
get translated into electrical signals within neurons, and
these signals are communicated to other neurons via
neurotransmitters.[3]

When it comes to depression and anxiety, the neurons and neurotransmitters are the primary components that are malfunctioning.
The chemicals being transferred from one neuron to the next are not
being identified or "absorbed," and therefore, the information is not
being passed along properly from one neuron to the next. Sometimes,
our bodies are lacking in the important "feel good" chemicals of serotonin and dopamine; other times, the chemicals are there but our neurons are not recognizing them. This is where medication comes into
play—when dealing with these specific mental illnesses. "When scientists discovered that the messages sent between neurons were based
on neurotransmitters sent from one neuron to the next, they began to
develop medications that could target this process. Many of the most
commonly used medications...such as Lexapro (escitalopram), Zoloft
(sertraline), Effexor (venlafaxine), and Cymbalta (duloxetine), were
designed to increase the amount of neurotransmitters available...as a
way of affecting circuits in certain areas of the brain."[4] Medication helps
your body absorb these important chemicals, giving you the emotional
and physical boost you need to counter depression and anxiety. Understanding what is happening inside your mind and body is a crucial part
of approaching mental illness in an educated and informed way.

What's Happening in My Body?

Not only are the chemicals in your brain being impacted, but
depression and anxiety also have a significant impact on your body.
In fact, many of the symptoms that tend to define depression and

anxiety are symptoms that manifest themselves physically. In fact, for some people, the physical symptoms begin long before the emotional symptoms.

Trey was a young man in his thirties who worked as a surgery technician in a hospital. One day during a surgical procedure, he started to feel dizzy. His entire body began to sweat, and he felt extremely nauseous. His heart rate spiked, and he felt like he was going to faint. He pushed through the last few minutes of the procedure and then bolted out of the room to find a bathroom. *What is happening?* he wondered. He thought he might be coming down with a terrible flu, so he headed home for the day. But within hours, he started feeling back to normal.

The next day at work, the episode happened again. And again the day after that. Soon, Trey was too fearful and anxious to go to work, so he took a week off. He wanted to give his body some time to heal from this strange virus he had. He felt much better after the week was over, but Monday morning found his body feeling miserable and in the exact same place that he started. After a series of appointments with medical doctors, Trey ended up in my counseling office thanks to a referral from his doctor. He still didn't understand what was happening in his body, but now he wondered if anxiety might be the cause. Over the course of the next few months, I helped Trey understand that mental health issues often strike with physical symptoms. And I encouraged him that if he could get to the root of his emotional and mental struggles, he could make a great impact on the physical symptoms that they induced. Sure enough, Trey found that to be a reality in his life. And as he identified the mental and emotional components that were impacting him and found solutions to those things, his physical symptoms subsided, and he started to gain back control in an area that had once felt so completely out of control.

There's an undeniable link between physical symptoms and mental health struggles. In fact, *psychosomatic* is a very common word we use as counselors that refers to real physical symptoms that are induced or caused by mental or emotional struggles rather than by an underlying physical illness or issue. Psychosomatic symptoms are important to recognize and understand because they point to the mental and emotional struggles going on underneath the surface. One study showed that adolescents who displayed a higher level of psychosomatic symptoms had a higher chance of developing a mental illness later in adulthood.[5] Another study analyzed the psychosomatic symptoms of teens who were facing bullying in school.[6] Those who were bullied had significantly higher odds of displaying psychosomatic symptoms including things like headache, backache, and sleeplessness. Our body has a powerful way of turning our mental and emotional struggles into physical ones because the neurotransmitters we talked about earlier impact every part of our being: mental, emotional, and physical.

Psychosomatic symptoms can be hard to identify because they often have a lot in common with diagnosable physical ailments and can in fact overlap. You can feel fatigue as a symptom of a virus, but you can also feel fatigue as a psychosomatic symptom of depression. Another fascinating study found that in the case of 1,000 new patients presenting with a total of 567 complaints of new physical symptoms such as dizziness, back pain, numbness, and weight loss, only 16 percent of them were found to have an actual diagnosable physical cause.[7] This doesn't conclude that 84 percent of these cases were psychosomatic, but it does mean that in cases with an unknown physical cause, it's important to be aware that mental and emotional struggles could be a potential underlying issue.

Another study found that in a group of patients presenting with physical symptoms, 20 percent of the patients came out with a diagnosis of *somatization*, meaning their physical symptoms were a result of underlying mental and emotional struggles versus an actual physical diagnosis.[8] Not only that, but the patients who were diagnosed with somatization actually had twice the amount of annual medical care costs than their nonsomatizing peers. Failing to understand the connection of mental and emotional struggles on your physical health can be costly—physically, mentally, and financially. This is why it's important to work alongside a medical professional if you're feeling any of the following symptoms on a regular basis:

- Fatigue
- Headaches
- Body aches
- Tingling in your arms or legs
- Digestive struggles
- Palpitations
- Sweating
- Brain fog
- Dizziness
- Swelling
- Impotence
- Weight loss or weight gain
- Shortness of breath
- Chest pain
- Insomnia
- Abdominal pain

This list represents some of the real physical symptoms a person can experience that may actually be psychosomatic symptoms caused by mental and emotional struggles. We'll hit this topic a little deeper in the next chapter about trauma and the body, but for now it's important to simply be aware that mental health struggles can have a genuine impact on our body because there are far too many false ideas about the impact and reality of mental illness.

Lies We Believe About Mental Illness

"True believers don't suffer from depression."

His false statement rang in my ear like a noisy gong and then hung in the air like smoke, waiting to be cleared away. I wasn't exactly sure how this conversation had started, but one thing led to another, and here I was with this visitor, who happened to be a pastor, and a small group of men and women discussing the existence of depression among Christians.

It would have been a hard conversation for anyone to have, but for me, it was excruciating. Because little did this visitor know that I was only now emerging from the terrible pit of depression myself. Little did he know that for me this conversation was personal because I'd felt like I'd just been to hell and back. Little did he know that my heart had wrestled and my body had collapsed under the pressure of depression. But that Jesus had held me the whole way through.

It breaks my heart to hear the myths and lies that Christians believe about depression and mental illness in general, and the shame that can be felt surrounding this topic. As I've interacted with more and more people on this topic, I've noticed that there are a few false ideas that continue to be perpetuated among believers. First and foremost is the false notion that you must be "weak" if you struggle with mental illness, as though your struggle is a reflection of your strength. Second, and one that I hear most often, is that a struggle with mental illness signifies a lack of faith or a problem in your walk with the Lord. Third, a false statement that tends to circulate among Christians is that the only thing you need to get through the struggle is prayer and God's Word. These statements couldn't be farther from the truth and cause so much damage inside people who are struggling. If you've ever heard or said any of the false statements above, here's what you really need to understand:

Your Struggle Is Not a Reflection of Your Strength

Your struggle does not indicate a weakness; in fact, those who struggle with mental health issues are usually the strongest. If life is a journey, those who are living with the hardships of mental health issues are the ones who are living life with an extra 50 pounds of burden on their shoulders, yet still taking the same steps as the person next door. Steps that reflect faithfulness, steps that reflect hope, and steps that reflect remarkable and courageous strength.

It's not whether or not you struggle that sets you apart; it's how you choose to handle the struggle.

Strength doesn't mean a lack of struggle, strength means getting through each day, even if that means getting dressed is all you do. Strength means asking for help. Strength means understanding your limitations and resetting your expectations during times of struggle. Strength means hearing the words of discouragement, yet choosing not to believe them. Strength means clinging to the truth. Strength means believing there is a light at the end of the tunnel, even when you can't see it. And ultimately, strength means recognizing that when we are feeling weak, there is One who makes us strong (2 Corinthians 12:9-11). When God is our strength, nothing and no one can stop us.

Your Struggle Is Not a Reflection of Your Faith

Not only is it false to believe that struggling with mental health issues is a reflection of your faith, but it's the antithesis of the entire message of Christ. As believers, we are never promised a pain-free, disease-free, struggle-free life. In fact, Jesus reminds us that in this world we will struggle (John 16:33). But in our struggle, we're promised a Savior, a Comforter, and a Friend. I look back at the hardest moments I have faced

> The struggle has been the catalyst for even deeper faith.

with depression and anxiety, and I see Jesus right by my side. My ever-present help in time of need (Psalm 46:1).

I remember crying out one night and feeling all alone, and just then God's presence overwhelmed me. Just when I needed it the most. Mental health struggles have nothing to do with lack of faith; in fact, for me and for so many others, the struggle has been the catalyst for even deeper faith. Because some days, in the hardest moments, faith was the only thing I had to hold on to.

Your Struggle Can Be Alleviated

Through my journey of depression and anxiety, I've learned that faith and action go hand in hand. One fuels the other. When we have faith, *we move*. When Jesus healed the paralytic at the pool of Bethesda, He told him to "get up...and walk" (John 5:8). Walking while paralyzed doesn't seem possible—just as impossible as it often seems to be able to "live" while struggling with mental illness. But Jesus reaches out His hand and tells us to *get up and walk*. Take the next step. Move the part of your body that you believe to be dead and dying. Take action. And trust God to give you the strength you need to take that next step. Taking action in this area of our life means understanding the role that counseling and medication play in alleviating our struggles. They're primary means of taking initiative toward mental health, and they're effective![9]

Just as we would never shame a cancer patient or a diabetic for their hurting bodies, we need to shift our perspective to see mental illness as a struggle of the brain and body. Only then will we be able to treat it in a proper way. There are many causes to mental illness, and whether it's rooted in trauma, hormones, chemical imbalance, or stress, it seeps into every part of our life. Our perspective of mental health illness needs to change so that we can learn to embrace and support those in it, pushing them toward healing instead of pushing them away.

Hope and Healing

My deepest prayer is that, as a body of believers, our attitudes would shift and our hearts would change as we face this important issue—that we would create an environment where we embrace and encourage those who are struggling with mental illness and in pain, rather than pushing them away. Some ways that we can begin to do that is by increasing awareness and then understanding that there is hope for healing, and it's often found in a combination of the following things: therapy, medication, and lifestyle changes.

Therapy

When you hear the word *therapy* or its synonym *psychotherapy*, what comes to mind? Hopefully, it's not an image of a bland office with a therapist scribbling notes while the client lies on a couch and shares his deepest, darkest fears. We've come a long way with our view of therapy, and I'm grateful for the fact that I see the stigma starting to fade with each passing year. Therapy is a profound experience, unlike anything else, guiding you through the difficult emotions and hard experiences in a hope-filled way. And not only that, but it's proven to be effective as a primary treatment method for people struggling with mental illness.[10] In fact, it's just as effective as medication when it comes to treating mild to moderate mental illness. There are several types of therapy from Cognitive Behavioral Therapy, to Solution Focused therapy, to Dialectical Behavioral Therapy, to EMDR and everything in between. Your therapist can talk you through what each type of therapy looks like and which one would be the most effective for your situation.

Take the next step by finding a counselor who is a good fit for you and what you're going through. Search for someone who is a licensed professional counselor but also a believer in Christ. There are plenty of Christian therapists to choose from, so it's important to read their biographies and get an idea of their area of expertise. Some counselors even welcome an introductory phone call where you can ask questions and get a feel for your connection before you schedule your first appointment. I'd also recommend that you give therapy time to work. It's not an overnight process, and I always suggest a minimum of six sessions to get a good idea of the connection you have with your counselor and whether or not it's a good match. Sometimes, it may take a trial or two to find a counselor that you connect with, but it's always worth the time and investment because it will have a tremendous impact on your mental health and well-being.

I remember one woman, Sarah, who told me through tears, "Therapy saved my life." She said that at our very last counseling appointment after one year of meeting regularly. The tears were a mix of elation for the hardships she had conquered, and sadness that we would no longer be meeting again. I felt the same mixture of emotions in my own heart.

She had come into counseling as a cynical young woman, broken from a traumatic past, struggling with major depression, and on the brink of taking her own life. Through the process of therapy, her eyes were opened to understanding and differentiating between the things she had control over and the things she didn't. She was empowered and strengthened. She worked hard on healing her past wounds, reformulating her identity, and learning how to deal with the difficult emotions in a productive way. She did the hard work of healing, and I had the honor of watching her become healthier and healthier with each passing month. Not only did Sarah work through counseling and come out healthier on the other side, but she was inspired to do the same for others. She enrolled in her first graduate school classes and began the journey of becoming a professional counselor herself. She wanted to give the gift of therapy to others.

> There's a stronger, healthier, better version of you waiting on the other side.

Don't let cynicism, fear, or apprehension stop you from giving yourself the gift of healing. Try counseling, and if you've tried it before, give it another chance. Allow God to use this healing relationship to transform and change you. Trust me when I say this: There's a stronger, healthier, better version of you waiting on the other side.

Medication

I was born into a medical home. I grew up seeing firsthand that medicine is a gift from God. Being a doctor's daughter, I've watched modern medicine decrease the risk of stroke and heart attacks, bring people into remission from cancer, and cure the most vicious infections. In fact, modern medicine has saved the lives of many people in my family and extended family, including my mother, who suffers from Type II diabetes. Every day, she faithfully takes her insulin—a little vial of medication that is literally keeping her alive. Needless to say, I'm beyond grateful for medication.

But not everyone feels the same way about medication, particularly when it comes to psychopharmacotherapy (medications that help the mind). Something about the word *antidepressant* strikes panic in some of the seemingly most levelheaded people, especially Christians. I've been in numerous counseling sessions in which I brought up the recommendation to consider pairing therapy with medication, and the stares that shot back at me from the other side of the room looked as if I had just used the word *voodoo*. When it comes to mental health, there is such an illogical fear of medication that wreaks havoc on the lives of so many people.

Earlier, I explained how some of these medications work, and why they're an important part of healing for many people. They bring your body back into balance when it has been hijacked by high levels of stress hormones (cortisol and adrenaline) and an imbalance of your feel-good chemicals (serotonin and dopamine). Not only that, but they have been proven to be just as effective as therapy, and the mixture of therapy paired with medication has been proven to be the most effective combination in dealing with mental illness.[11]

But I have to admit, I do understand a bit of hesitation and fear. I felt it myself. In fact, I clearly remember the first time my dad recommended I try an antidepressant. "ME?!?" I shot back at him. *But, but, but...I'm a licensed counselor! I help people deal with depression and anxiety. I give people strategies. Why would I need medication?* Those were the thoughts that went through my mind, and I dragged my feet on the decision until I realized how much my mental health struggles were impacting my body. I wasn't sleeping, I wasn't eating, I had lost 15 pounds in a very short time period, I was crying constantly, I had no energy, I couldn't concentrate, and my brain felt like it was living in a fog. My body was failing me, and I needed something to help my body. When I have a cold, I don't hesitate to take cold medicine. When I get a migraine, I turn to medication the second I feel it coming on. So why was this any different? I'd always taught this exact concept to my clients, but now it was time to live it out.

And I am so glad I did! Friends, within a few weeks, my body started feeling back to normal. By the three-month mark, I was feeling 100 percent back to myself. The depression and anxiety had lifted. The cortisol levels from the stress I was facing had leveled out, and the serotonin and dopamine levels that had been completely ransacked by my body began to realign and rebalance. My body was "resetting" in a way that I couldn't get it to do on my own. That was the first time I went on medication, and eventually I was able to wean off it and resume life as normal.

Fast-forward to last summer, when I went through another terrible spell of depression and anxiety. I could hardly function for two weeks, and this time it didn't take me long to decide I needed to go back on medication. In fact, at this point, I would have eaten rabbit poop if I knew it would help me feel better. With the help of my thoughtful and caring doctor, I started Lexapro to help bring my serotonin levels back to where they needed to be. She also gave me a prescription of Xanax (an antianxiety medicine that's meant to be taken as needed to stop anxiety in the moment) to help me get through the first few weeks while I waited for the antidepressant to kick in. What a gift modern medicine can be! Within *hours*, the Xanax made an incredible difference in my life, and within weeks, thanks to the Lexapro, I started feeling back to myself. Depression and anxiety are often comorbid illnesses, meaning one usually comes with the other. Taking an antidepressant (an SSRI) is the go-to method for tackling both anxiety and depression, or either/or. Helping one almost always helps the other. I'm not saying that this is the healing combination of medications, because for everyone it looks different. You have to work with your doctor to find the medication that's going to work for you, and then you've got to commit to following their lead with how and when to take it.

People often worry about the side effects of these medications or worry that they'll build a dependency on them. For me, the side effects were mild, but I did feel an increase of anxiety for the first few days as my serotonin levels recalibrated (which is why the Xanax was important during that time), as well as some mild muscle twitching. And over the next 11 months, I put on a little bit more weight than usual. But to put things in perspective for you, I'd take those few days of mild discomfort and few extra pounds *any day* over the hell of deep depression and anxiety that I was dealing with. As I write this chapter, I'm feeling fantastic! With the help of my doctor, I was eventually able to slowly wean off the medication completely by dropping to half a dose, and then half of that as time passed and as my body returned to baseline. Most people need to be on medication for at least six months to a year to really gauge how it's helping them. In fact, the medicine often does not even take full effect until four to six weeks.

I was just thinking back to those terrible days this past summer and am so grateful for the gift of modern medicine, incredible doctors, and wonderful therapists. Thank You, Jesus! Don't be afraid to do what you need to do to get your body and mind back to where they need to be.

Lifestyle Changes

Lastly, it's important to know that there are ways to impact your brain chemistry and stabilize your mood just by changing your habits. Things like diet, exercise, and sleep can have a significant impact on your mental health. We're going to get to those in detail in chapter 10 about the body-mind connection because even small changes can have a big impact on your life.

Taking Inventory

When it comes to taking initiative in your mental health, what does the next step look like for you?

That next step might be reaching out to someone to let them know you're suffering.

It might mean walking into an emergency room and letting them know you don't think you're safe to be alone.

It might be setting up an appointment with your medical doctor to finally get to the bottom of all those symptoms you've been ignoring.

It might be seeing a psychiatrist and talking through medication options.

It might mean enrolling in professional counseling.

It might mean filling that prescription of antidepressants you've been debating if you should start taking.

It might mean asking for help while you focus on rest and recovery.

It might mean calling a suicide hotline.

It might mean all of the above.

Whatever it is, take the next step because there is absolutely no shame in seeking help and moving toward healing. Let me remind you that faith and action go hand in hand (James 2:26). When we begin to move, God begins to heal, and when God begins to heal, we begin to move. The key to pursuing mental health is to simply do the next thing. That, my friends, is what faith is all about.

God is with you on the mountaintop, and He's with you in the valley. Your one and only job right now is to do the next thing and step-by-step get yourself to a better place.

Journaling Questions: 5-Minute Mental Health Checkup

- Take a look at these common symptoms of anxiety and depression, and check off any you might be currently feeling:

  o ANXIETY

    - Excessive worry about a variety of topics
    - Worry that's hard to control

- Worry that comes with three or more of the following:

  - Restlessness
  - Fatigue
  - Difficulty concentrating
  - Irritability
  - Muscle aches or soreness
  - Difficulty sleeping
  - Other physical symptoms such as sweating or digestive problems

o DEPRESSION
  - Depressed mood
  - Decreased interest or pleasure in most activities
  - Weight changes (weight loss or weight gain)
  - Sleep disturbance (too much or too little)
  - Fatigue
  - Feelings of worthlessness or hopelessness
  - Difficulty concentrating
  - Recurring thoughts of death or suicide

If you checked off three or more on either list above, consider making an appointment to discuss your symptoms with your medical doctor and take the next steps toward mental health.

- Do I have any unexplained physical symptoms that could be linked to my mental health? If so, make a list of those symptoms.

- What are the lies that I have been taught or believed about mental health and mental illness?

- What is one next step that I can take in maintaining or pursuing mental health in my life?

9

Trauma Messes with Your Head

Peeling Back the Layers

Note: This chapter may be a trigger for anyone who has struggled with trauma, specifically in the form of a miscarriage. Please feel free to skip to page 185 of this chapter if reading this personal experience would bring up unnecessary pain.

Emergency surgery was the last thing I would have expected when I woke up that morning. I was eight weeks pregnant with our fourth child after delivering our third child only five months prior. To say a fourth pregnancy was an unexpected surprise would be an understatement. We were completely blindsided, and though we clearly know how pregnancies happen, we still couldn't quite make sense of this one. The timing just didn't seem to add up. Yet, this was our reality, and we embraced it with overwhelming joy.

Something instantly happens when you find out you're pregnant. When the initial shock (or the initial freaking out, in this case) wears off, you find that your heart has expanded, immediately making space to love in a way you never thought possible. Our hearts began preparing for the arrival of our fourth child.

It's amazing how there can be an intermingling of joy and pain all at the same time. You see, the six months prior to getting pregnant, our family had walked through the hardest experience of our entire lives. It's too personal and painful for me to share the details, but let me assure you that we had never gone through more uncertain and difficult times as we witnessed a loved one suffer immense and enduring pain. So, the unexpected feelings of joy at this new pregnancy were a breath of fresh air during a very dark time. But all of that changed within a matter of days.

I woke up one morning to spotting—a possible sign that I might be miscarrying this child inside my body. We didn't want to panic, as spotting can also be a routine part of pregnancy for some women. We had an important medical appointment scheduled for our middle son, so we decided that John would take the kids to the appointment while I went to see the obstetrician for a checkup.

The first thing they scheduled for me was a sonogram to check on the status of the baby. As the sonogram was being performed, I could tell by the somber look on the technician's face that something was wrong. I tried to make conversation, hoping that her responses could tell me something one way or another, but they didn't. She left the room, and I went into the bathroom to change back into my clothes. That's when I noticed I was bleeding even more.

My doctor confirmed the worst. We had lost the baby, and I was miscarrying. The bleeding was the beginning of the process, she explained, and I could go home to wait it out, or I could schedule surgery sometime in the next few days. It was too much to process right then and there, and I was flooded with emotions. I told her I would go home for now and then call back later to schedule surgery. But right as

I was about to get up, I noticed I was feeling light-headed. I asked for some water to drink before I got up to leave. Then, I remembered the bleeding from earlier, and right then and there I noticed that my body felt like it was losing more blood than felt normal. I mentioned it to her, and then asked if she would check me before I left.

The following moments will remain burned into my memory for the rest of my life. As I sat back, I suddenly began bleeding out in a way I never imagined possible. The doctor looked at me, her eyes filled with anxiety, and said with a calm but deadly serious voice, "Debra, you are severely hemorrhaging. This is serious. We need to go to emergency surgery *right now,* and we don't have time to waste. Here's your phone. I need you to call your husband and your family and tell them to come to the hospital immediately." I grabbed the phone with shaking hands, called my husband and then my dad, and somehow managed to explain to them that they needed to drive to the hospital immediately because I was going into emergency surgery. One of the strangest things is that I remember how calm my voice was. Partially, because I didn't want to cause them to panic, but partly because it felt like my life was flashing before my eyes, and my emotions didn't have time to catch up to what was happening. What I know now that I didn't know then is that I was minutes away from losing my life.

In the background, I heard the doctor yelling out into the hallway that there was an emergency, and within seconds, they brought me a wheelchair. When they sat me up, I saw that there was a tremendous amount of blood everywhere—so much blood that it looked like something out of a horror movie. I remember seeing it all but feeling removed from it, as though all of these things were happening to someone other than me. They helped me into a wheelchair, and that's when I remember I started to shake. My entire body began to shiver uncontrollably, and my teeth chattered to the point where I could hardly talk. I was losing so much blood so quickly that it was starting to impact my body temperature.

The doctor said she was going to wheel me to surgery herself, and within seconds we were speeding down a long, narrow hallway. Somehow, through it all, I felt calm. An indescribable calm. A calm that really didn't match the severity of the situation. I believe some of that calm came from my lack of awareness of what was really happening, as well as how quickly things happened, but the other component to the calm was Jesus. He was walking by my side, or should I say running next to my wheelchair, reminding me that I was not alone, that He was with me.

A flurry of things happened in the next few minutes, including a few kind nurses reciting the risks of surgery while quickly changing my shivering body into surgical attire, and then letting me know they would remove my wedding ring. Something about the act of taking off my ring really hit me: I was about to go into emergency surgery all by myself. Things progressed so quickly that my family hadn't had a chance to arrive at the hospital yet, and I was wheeled into surgery with only Jesus by my side.

The last thing I remember was seeing a room full of masked doctors and nurses quickly giving me an injection and asking me to count backwards. "Take good care of me, okay?" I managed to sleepily joke with one of my new masked friends in the room. "No, we're not going to take good care of you. We're going to take *excellent* care of you," he said back to me with a wink. Then, everything went dark.

I woke up in a small postoperative room and blinked a few times to see my husband standing by my side with a look of relief and joy on his face as he gave me a big kiss. My dad was there, too, talking to the doctor.

She looked at me and said, "You're one lucky lady. The stars aligned for you today."

"It wasn't the stars," I groggily told her. "It was the God who made the stars."

I knew God was good, sovereign, and trustworthy. Yet, deep down, the reality that I had lost my fourth child and almost lost my life that day hadn't quite settled in. That would come later. And in time, the trauma that I had experienced that day would begin to seep into my life in a way that I wasn't expecting.

≡

"Trauma cracks us open...so that the Holy Spirit can get in," Carolyn Weber said in her book about holy moments.[1] Trauma is always painful, and it breaks you. But it's in that brokenness that the Holy Spirit works. It's in that weakness that we are invited into the process of being made strong.

I didn't understand the extent of my brokenness the year I went through my traumatic miscarriage because God made humans to be resilient in the face of trauma; otherwise, we wouldn't survive it. Many times, we don't feel the effects of trauma in the midst of trauma. We only feel the effects later on—when time has passed, and life is safe and secure. It takes time for our emotions to catch up.

Think of soldiers who go off to war. While they're on the battlefield, they're in survival mode. The goal is to stay alive. They experience trauma on every level, but the time to process those atrocities is not while you're in the midst of them. The only thing you have time for during trauma is one thing and one thing alone: survival.

But when soldiers come home from war, and life begins to settle down, this is when their trauma begins to resurface. The body now has the time to process and deal with the horrific things it has experienced. Now that it has survived, it can begin to heal. This is why symptoms of post-traumatic stress disorder don't often happen on the battlefield. They happen afterward, when things are calm, safe, and steady.

My calm, safe, and steady came about two years after my traumatic experience. I was in the kitchen one day making the kids lunch, when suddenly, I felt light-headed. Looking back, I don't fully know what triggered that feeling. Realistically, it was probably because I hadn't eaten or had anything to drink that day, and it was near one o'clock in the afternoon. What's interesting about this sudden experience, though, is that the last time I felt light-headed was right before I went into emergency surgery. But to be honest, I didn't even think of that at the time because I was just focused on what was happening here and now. Though I wasn't *cognitively* aware of it, my body remembered what my brain could not. My body recognized that experience and went into fight-or-flight mode. I didn't recognize this at the time, but it's almost as if my body was saying, "Wait a second—you feel light-headed! Remember? You went through this right before you almost died! You better take it seriously this time! This is dangerous! This is life threatening!" Next thing you know, I was spiraling into anxiety. All my emotional alarms were firing at full speed. I started feeling shortness of breath, my heart rate skyrocketed, my entire body began to sweat, and I had to sit down immediately. I asked my daughter to bring me a glass of water as I tried to mask my anxiety. When I couldn't seem to get my body under control, I picked up the phone to call my husband. These are the times I'm grateful to God that I'm married to a doctor—and a calm one, at that. God knew what I needed.

John listened to my symptoms and assured me that they weren't alarming. Feeling dizzy makes sense when you haven't eaten all day, and all the other physical symptoms I was experiencing were likely anxiety. There was nothing urgent, he assured me. He suggested I go eat something and then lie down and call him back in 20 minutes to let him know how I was feeling. Sure enough, by that time I was starting to feel back to my normal self. I called him back to let him know, and then went about my day as though nothing had happened. But what I didn't realize is that was the beginning of an anxious response that would lead me to an anxious pattern that would me lead down the path of having a full-blown panic attack on a safari bus.

Your Body Remembers

Trauma is not a once-and-done experience. In fact, traumatic experiences make their way into our bodies by getting buried deep down in our brain, in a center of the brain called the amygdala. The amygdala is the part of our brain that is responsible for storing emotional memories—experiences that have triggered emotional responses. There are so many positive emotional memories that are stored in our amygdala, such as the smell of fresh cookies baking in the oven, that bring a flood of joyful warmth as they remind you of your mom making you an afterschool snack as a child. Or the feelings of love and appreciation that fill your heart when you look through old photos of your wedding, birthdays, and other significant experiences.

> Trauma is not a once-and-done experience.

Your amygdala has the extremely important job of remembering strong emotions. Significant relationships are made as a result of our emotional memories—significant feelings we have experienced over the years. If the amygdala didn't remember emotions, you would feel nothing when you walked into a room and saw your spouse. But instead, you feel the love and appreciation that has built up over time, the sum of millions of emotional memories. You couldn't name every single memory in the moment, but you don't have to because your body remembers.

On the other hand, just as the amygdala stores positive emotional memories, it also stores negative emotional memories. When a person goes through a difficult or traumatic experience that causes significant distress, the body remembers. Take, for instance, Tony, a middle-aged man who gets into a terrible car accident as a result of someone running a red light. He's rushed to the emergency room by ambulance and undergoes many long months of recovery and rehabilitation. When Tony gets home from the hospital, he notices that every time he gets into a car, he's suddenly filled with feelings of anxiety. His body remembers the feelings of terror that accompanied the car accident and makes the association that a vehicle always represents danger.

Or consider the story of Amanda, a young wife who got a devastating phone call informing her of the sudden, tragic death of her husband one day while she was at home doing laundry and listening to orchestra music in the background. Her body made the association between the tragic, sorrowful feelings she felt during that phone call and the music that was playing in the background. As time passed, she noticed a strong aversion anytime she heard classical music. It would bring feelings of sorrow and anxiety, without her awareness of why this was happening. Her body remembered what her mind did not.

Not only does the amygdala store emotional memories, but it also helps us to respond to emotional cues. "The amygdala's central location in the brain places it in an advantageous position to influence other parts of the brain that can change essential bodily functions in a fraction of a second...All of these changes are part of the fight, flight, or freeze response...When this reaction is needed, we consider it a lifesaving event. But if [it] overreacts, it can set off a full-blown panic attack when no logical reason for fear exists."[2] The body remembers. It remembers, and it responds. God gave us such a gift in this reaction because it is this fight, flight, or freeze response that has saved countless lives over time. But it is also this same response that can overreact or sound a "false alarm," causing a negative impact on our mental health if we're not aware of it.

False Alarms

I started experiencing these overreactions or false alarms about a year or so after my traumatic miscarriage. It started with feeling faint in the kitchen that day, but then it began to happen more often and quickly impacted other parts of my life. Soon, anytime I would feel any sort of physical ailment, my anxiety would begin to spiral without my permission. I would go into fight-or-flight mode, truly believing that something terrible might be happening to me. My body remembered my trauma and continued to respond to any sign of physical ailment as though it were a traumatic experience.

I started feeling uncomfortable anytime I was in a closed environment, where I wouldn't be able to "get out" if I needed help. Driving through a long tunnel on the way to New York City with my husband one evening, my anxiety came out of nowhere, and I felt my body shutting down, until we got to the end of the tunnel, and I felt like I could breathe again. At church, I started feeling the need to sit at the end of the aisle and near the door because I was worried that I might not feel well and needed a plan for escape.

All of this culminated the day I was sitting on an open safari bus, in 96-degree weather on Labor Day weekend. I started feeling hot and light-headed. The scorching sun was beating down on my head, causing droplets of sweat to run down the side of my face. I looked around me, and I realized that I wasn't feeling well, and there was no escape. There were wild animals all around me and no way to get off this bus. My amygdala kicked into full gear, causing every part of my body to go into fight-or-flight mode. My heart felt like it was pounding out of my chest. It was so loud I could hear it in my ears. My body felt like it was on fire, and I was dripping sweat as though I had just run a marathon. My breathing felt labored, and I felt like my throat was closing, and soon I wouldn't be able to breathe at all. I felt like I could die on this safari bus. The next few minutes were like a nightmare—one that no one could see or understand but me. I wanted to scream and run, but I couldn't. My body felt so bad, but my mind felt even worse. Everything felt like it was on fire, and there was nothing I could do.

If you've ever had a panic attack before, you know that most of the time they only last a few minutes—but those few minutes often feel like an eternity. The minutes of panic on the safari bus felt like the longest few minutes of my life. Trauma has a way of skewing everything—from your emotional response, to your awareness of time and space, to your logic and reason.

At the time of my panic attack on the safari bus, I hadn't yet made the connection that my body was experiencing these physical and emotional symptoms as a result of my past trauma. I didn't realize that my body was overreacting to the traumatic experience of my past with hypervigilance in the present. It took time and dealing with about six months of feelings of heightened anxiety and panic before I was able to step back and put the pieces together. My training as a counselor helped me begin to look at the situation objectively, realizing that these anxiety responses were my amygdala's attempt at keeping me safe from harm—but there really was no harm this time around. Now that I understood what was happening, I wanted to find a way out of this cycle. So, I invited my friend, longtime mentor, and licensed psychologist, Dr. Hamon, to walk with me through this hard time and help me understand, process, as well as have power over my amygdala response. There were a lot of things at play in my mental health at this stage of my life, including past trauma, hormonal changes, and current life stress, and I needed someone to help me come up with a plan and keep me moving toward healing.

I've said it before, and I'll say it again, but this is why professional counseling is such an important part of moving toward mental health. If you've experienced any type of past trauma that you've yet to process with a professional counselor, don't wait one more day. There are so many negative emotional and physical responses to trauma that you could be living with and tolerating without even realizing it. Start the process of healing because it's truly just that: a process. The faster you begin, the faster you move toward healing.

Healing Happens in Layers

Healing from trauma isn't a once-and-done experience because trauma gets buried deep down inside. Just as it takes months or even years sometimes for the effects of trauma to make their way into your life, it often takes months and years to peel back the layers one at a time and receive healing in each of the different parts of your life. It's a refining process that happens one layer at a time. As you heal in one area, the Lord reveals a new area that you're ready to heal from as well. You should never see it as a setback when something new comes up that you need to heal from; instead, you should see it as the Lord refining you one layer at a time, taking each part of the trauma and turning it into triumph.

I remember one evening when another "layer" of healing happened in my life. I was getting ready for bed, and I found myself having a flashback of the night of my emergency surgery. Let me take a moment to remind you that flashbacks are not signs that you're backtracking— in fact, they're just the opposite. Flashbacks are a sign that your body is finally ready to recall the hard things you've been through. It's a sign that you're strong enough to handle the memories now, so they come back up again as an opportunity to revisit the experience and receive healing. One layer at a time.

> Flashbacks are a sign that you're strong enough to handle the memories.

As I was experiencing this flashback, my mind kept going back to the tremendous amount of blood that I saw all around me when I sat up that day. I could hear the doctor saying, "We need to go to emergency surgery, now!" echoing in my mind as the entire experience raced through my mind again like a movie on fast-forward. I then flashed back to hearing my doctor say that I was literally minutes from dying that day. All of a sudden, I heard the Lord interrupt my thought process. It wasn't an audible voice, but it was loud and clear in my mind. The most interesting thing about this interruption is that it didn't match the tone of my flashback. The flashback was sad, scary, and filled with grief. But the Lord's voice broke through the darkness of this flashback with unexpected laughter. Not a cynical laughter, but an endearing, comforting one that helped me see the situation from His perspective. I heard Him say with a lighthearted chuckle, *You didn't almost die that day. That doctor doesn't know what I know, and you were the furthest thing from dying. I had you in My hands.* He was telling me, *Don't let trauma fool you,*

Deb. Don't give your experience so much power over your life. My reality is greater than your reality. Trust Me more than you trust your reality.

He interrupted my traumatic flashback with His healing truth—a truth that I desperately needed to hear. A truth that reminded me that I was alive and well today not because of coincidence or well-timed emergency surgery or minutes that could have led to a morgue. I was alive and well not—like the doctor had said—because the stars aligned, but because of God's undeniable sovereignty. I was alive because of God's hand. Because of His plan. A plan that no trauma or tragedy could stop. I had to begin to face the trauma in my life with this truth.

Facing Trauma with Truth

Trauma has the ability to change the story you tell yourself. It has the power to take a good story and taint it with fear, hopelessness, and disillusionment. In chapter 7 we talked about the power of our thoughts and the importance of having an awareness and taking ownership of the story you tell yourself. But without our permission, trauma can take our story and scribble all over it with the black marker of pain. It can be hard to take ownership of our story when we can't always tell the difference between truth and trauma. This is why we can't expect ourselves to be able to walk through trauma alone. We need help—the help of a professional counselor—to be able to step back from the story and separate the voice of trauma from the voice of truth.

I remember counseling a 30-year-old woman named Heather, who came to my office after living through a severe trauma many months before. Listening to her story was like hearing the plotline from a horror movie. She was taking the bus to work one day when she was held at gunpoint by a man sitting next to her. He quietly held the gun to her side and whispered in her ear that she needed to follow him off the bus. No one around them noticed the deadly exchange. At the next bus stop, he grabbed her arm, and they walked to an alley where she was blindfolded as they walked to an unknown location. For the next seven days, Heather was tied to a chair in a garage and instantly became a prisoner to this evil man, who caused unspeakable trauma in her life. On day seven, she noticed that in her captor's drunkenness that day, he had left the garage partially open, so she decided to attempt an escape. Heather was able to free herself and quietly sneak away while her captor slept. She ran straight to the busiest street she could find, was picked up by a good citizen, and was immediately taken to the police where she reported this heinous crime against her. The man was captured that same day and was eventually sentenced to many years in jail.

But knowing her captor was captured didn't even begin to heal the trauma she had experienced. A few months after her experience, she started to notice that everything in her life had changed. She was filled with anxiety on a regular basis and found herself experiencing severe panic at the thought of taking public transportation. She couldn't sleep at night due to the nightmares she was experiencing, and she lost her appetite. Even when she was safe in the comfort of her own home, her body remained hypervigilant. Trauma had scribbled all over the story of her life, and she was now convinced that nothing was safe, and no one could be trusted. It began to impact her closest relationships, and she found herself pulling away from the people who loved her the most.

In our counseling sessions, I focused on helping Heather differentiate trauma from truth. We had to walk through those hard experiences, acknowledge them, feel their pain, but then determine that those experiences would not define every other part of her life. Without going into too much detail, let me explain that there are many different types of therapy that can be used to help rewrite the story of trauma—from cognitive-behavioral therapy, to EMDR, to psychodynamic therapy, to exposure therapy. For Heather, healing came through visiting and revisiting her traumatic events through detailed storytelling and exposure therapy. Each time through the experience allowed her to see more truth, to have more strength, and for the trauma to have less power in her life. Eventually, it meant even going back *physically* to those hard places in order to allow herself to build new experiences—better experiences—and to continue to face her trauma with truth. The truth was, she had gone through a horrific experience, but that experience did not define the entirety of her life. The truth is, she is safe, she is victorious, and she has won.

The Different Strokes of Trauma

Trauma doesn't have to be as severe as Heather's story for it to have a great impact on the story of your life. Its strokes can scribble over your story in many ways. For some, trauma could mean dealing with the sexual or physical abuse you've endured in the past at the hands of a stranger—or even worse, someone you trusted and loved. For others, trauma is growing up with an emotionally unhealthy parent who neglected you, ignored you, or shamed you. Maybe it comes in the form of an alcoholic parent, who scribbled over the story of your life with rage, deceit, and emotional instability. Maybe trauma comes in the form of a toxic boyfriend or girlfriend, a severe car accident or life-threatening illness, or the unexpected or tragic death of a loved one. All these things have one thing in common because trauma is defined by one thing and one thing alone: loss. The loss of love, the loss of innocence, the loss of stability, the loss of control, the loss of safety and security, the loss of justice, the loss of a loved one, the loss of your health, your marriage, your job, your child, or your parent. The list could go on and on because there are so many forms of loss that can impact your heart and life. Loss leads to distress, and distress leads to trauma. The most fascinating thing about trauma is that it doesn't even have to happen *to you* for you to experience it. Watching someone else go through tragedy and loss can also cause personal trauma in your life. Trauma comes in many different strokes, and recognizing those strokes is such an important part of healing because when we recognize them, we can begin to write over them with truth.

Mindfulness: Focusing on Truth

One of the most purposeful ways of fixing our hearts and minds on truth is a practice called mindfulness. Mindfulness is essentially a stilling of our minds and a focusing of our attention. It gives us the opportunity to take inventory of our thoughts and then to take ownership of them. God's Word reminds us of the importance of taking every thought captive and making it obedient to Christ (2 Corinthians 10:5). This is essentially the attitude of mindfulness and its synonym: meditation.

For many Christians, the words *mindfulness* or *meditation* might come with a negative connotation or an assumption that the practice is associated with Eastern religions. But mindfulness and meditation have been part of the Christian tradition dating back to the words of Scripture. We're instructed to "meditate" on God's Word day and night (Joshua 1:8). Theologian J.I. Packer writes that this practice is...

> ...a lost art today, and Christian people suffer grievously from their ignorance of the practice. Meditation is the activity of calling to mind, and thinking over, and dwelling on, and applying to oneself, the various things that one knows about the works and ways and purposes and promises of God. It is an activity of holy thought, consciously performed in the presence of God, under the eye of God, by the help of God, as a means of communion with God.[3]

In Christian mindfulness, we're meditating on God's truth. And that is what makes all the difference. We're giving ourselves a chance to take captive the thoughts that might be harming us and to replace them with God's healing truth. We're renewing our minds and, according to the book of Romans, that process is transformational (Romans 12:2). Mindfulness is a practice of fixing our hearts on right now—not the past, not the future, but the moment. This moment. It's an act of centering our hearts and our minds on the here and now—because that is exactly where God resides. He is the I AM. Present tense. Not the "I was" or the "I will be," but the great I AM (Exodus 3:14).

When a person walks through trauma, they can find that being present or mindful of the moment becomes a very difficult and hard-to-achieve experience. If mindfulness is the act of being aware of how we feel and what we're experiencing, many times trauma causes us to run from those feelings and experiences because we (consciously or unconsciously) don't want to risk feeling or experiencing something difficult again. As the authors of one study put it,

> Part of the process [of a traumatic experience] becomes increasing use of a variety of avoidant behaviors. Some examples of these that we commonly observe include efforts to suppress intrusive thoughts, removal of one-self from situations that elicit negative private experiences, substance use, and emotional numbing. This avoidance of painful internal psychological experiences represents the antithesis of mindful behavior and it becomes a persistent strategy that is maintained by conditioning processes.[4]

This response of avoidance not only hinders mindfulness, but it hinders healing. Running from the present is a counterproductive response. It avoids healing rather than invites healing. In fact, one study found that those who avoided the difficult emotions and experiences ended up experiencing stronger symptoms of panic than those who did not.[5]

Practicing deliberate mindfulness has been shown to be an effective method in decreasing symptoms of trauma and dealing with difficult emotions. "Mindfulness...encourages acceptance, rather than rigid avoidance of one's experiences."[6] It brings healing by allowing us to be focused on the present rather than ruled by the pain of the past or the fear of the future. A great resource on the practice of mindfulness and meditation is a book called *Holy Noticing* by Charles Stone.[7] Not only does he lay out the biblical and scientific foundations for the practice of mindfulness, but he also offers a practical method of engaging in mindfulness. In his book, he offers a method that he calls the BREATHe method, which stands for:

- **B**ody—being aware of your physical body states and sensations

- Relationships—assessing the health of your relationships
- Environment—taking notice of your current surroundings, including sights, sounds, smells, and God's creation
- Afflictive emotions or Affect—acknowledging how you're currently feeling
- Thoughts—being conscious of your current thoughts
- Heart—paying attention to the state of your spiritual life and the Holy Spirit's whisperings or impressions on your heart
- Engage—engaging the world like Christ, practicing holy noticing in the mundane, the everyday, the ordinary

The act of mindfulness is essentially taking a "scan" of your entire body from the inside out, from top to bottom, stopping to pay special attention to areas of struggle. When I'm walking my clients through a traditional mindfulness exercise, I always make sure we begin the mindfulness process by closing our eyes as a method of focus and then paying extra attention to our breathing patterns as we begin to tune in to the physical components of our body. Incorporating Scripture during this time can mean taking any verse or phrase from God's Word that is meaningful to you and integrating it into your time of breathing. In *Holy Noticing*, Charles Stone recommends using the phrase "Holy Spirit" on your breath-in, "Breathe on me," on your breath-out.

The act of taking control of your breathing, in and of itself, has a great impact on your mind and body. In fact, breathing techniques are one of the most commonly used methods of reducing stress and dealing with anxiety because, as we mentioned in earlier chapters, anxiety has a tendency to hijack your sympathetic system and cause your breathing to be uncontrolled and haphazard, which then has a negative impact on how you're feeling in other areas of your body.

The next step in the practice of mindfulness is to take inventory of your body with regard to your muscles. From the top of your head to the bottom of your toes, with your eyes still closed, you allow your focus to spotlight every muscle and take inventory of any tension you might be carrying in your body. I have a tendency to carry all my stress in my upper back and shoulders. It often leads to headaches and back-aches because I tense those muscles when I'm stressed without even realizing it. It's only when I pay close attention to those parts of my body that I can begin to relax and relieve them. One practice I love in *Holy Noticing*, is the practice of not simply taking note of your muscle tension as you scan through each body part, but then going the next step and thanking God for that part of your body, ending with this simple prayer: *Lord, thank You for giving me my body. I am fearfully and wonderfully made. I yield it to You today as a living sacrifice.*[8]

Once you've controlled your breathing and relaxed your muscles, it's time to take inventory from the inside out. It's time to notice. This is where the BREATHe method mentioned above can be especially helpful, and I highly recommend you take the time to read through the entire book as you develop the art of mindfulness as a regular prac-tice in your life.[9]

What type of things can God bring to your attention when you take the time to notice? What problem spots in your body, in your feelings, in your thoughts, in your environment, in your relationships, or in your behaviors might He ask you to renew as He leads you into transformation? What old patterns of thinking does He want to inter-rupt as you take the time to meditate on Him and on His truth? How might He begin to write over the tragedy and trauma of your past with the truth and hope of His presence? The act of mindfulness and medi-tation is an invitation to align our hearts with His. To see how He sees. Feel what He feels. Hear what He hears. Notice what He notices. To face our trauma with truth.

Truth Journaling

If trauma is a topic that you can identify with, I want to encourage you to start something I call truth journaling. We've used the healing effect of journaling throughout each chapter of this book so far, and this chapter is no different. One way to face our trauma with truth is simply to write it out. As you go through the practice of mindfulness, take the time to write down the things God brings to your attention. On one side of your journal, write down the effects, impact, and outcome of your trauma. Write out the hard things that continue to plague you with fear or instill panic in your heart. Make a list of the dark places you tend to find your mind wandering to from the past or the fears you have for the future. Read over that list with a heart of acknowledgment and acceptance of the hard things you've been through. But don't stop there.

On the other side of your journal, I want you to focus on the truth. The truth of who God says you are and what He is speaking into your heart. If you don't feel Him speaking truth into your life right away, that's okay. Leave it blank, and give it time and space, inviting God to give you a truth for every trauma. The truth may not come in the form of an answer, but it will always come in the form of renewal. The trauma will be made new. Let us hold on to the promise of 2 Corinthians 5:17: "If anyone is in Christ, the new creation has come: The old has gone, the new is here!"

If you came to my house someday and opened the bottom drawer of my nightstand, there you'd find my trusty journal. And if you cracked open that black leather journal, maybe you'd find a tear-stained page that had the word *TRAUMA* written in big, bold, black ink strokes. Underneath that treacherous word, you might find a sentence scribbled in smaller, sloppier handwriting that acknowledged the pain and hardships I have faced. Maybe the sentence would read something like this: *I was minutes away from losing my life in a terrifying, traumatic miscarriage.*

But if you looked to the other side of the page, there you would also find another big, bold word. Even bigger and bolder than the last word. This time, in big, bold, black ink strokes, you'd see the word **TRUTH**. And under that word you'd read a new sentence. A sentence that reflects the time when God interrupted my traumatic experience with His truth. And that sentence would read: *My life was never at stake because I was in the safe hands of the God who numbers my days and plans my steps. And one, joy-filled day when I meet Jesus face-to-face, I will be reunited with the precious baby I held in my womb, but never in my arms.*

That, my friends, is when trauma comes face-to-face with truth. It doesn't undo the pain of the past, but it gives us perspective and perseverance for today. It doesn't undo the tears of yesterday, but it allows us to see triumph in today. It doesn't erase the hurts of our childhoods, but it allows us to find healing in today. It allows us to center our hearts and minds on what is, rather than what could be. It keeps us fixated on the present—the one and only thing on which we can truly make an impact.

> The truth may not come in the form of an answer, but it will always come in the form of renewal.

The journey of replacing my trauma with truth has had an indescribable impact on my life. I've recognized the dark strokes of trauma and have begun to rewrite the story with the brushstrokes of truth. Truth that shines a light on my past and offers hope for the present. I've learned to hold on to the reminder that even when my body may fail me, my God does not. And as a result, the anxiety and panic my body used to feel at the first sign of physical ailment has subsided and diminished with time. I've found freedom.

He Knows Trauma

I cannot help but find comfort in knowing that not only is facing trauma a common part of the human experience (1 Corinthians 10:13), but it's something our very own Savior went through Himself. As He hung there on a cross, bruised and bleeding, tortured and terrorized, abandoned by His closest friends, misunderstood and forsaken, left to hang in shame for something He didn't do, He had to face His own trauma. I can only imagine the thoughts that could have been looming in His mind in those awful moments. I know what I would have been thinking as the agony of trauma wrote over the story—the story I thought I knew. Trauma says:

Rejection has arrived.

Disappointment echoes.

Fear reigns.

Depression sinks in.

Worry abounds.

Guilt destroys.

Anger grows.

Hopelessness encompasses.

Sorrow surrounds.

Death wins.

But the story was not over. Not for Him and not for us. Because in Christ we will always be victorious in the end. Trauma does not have the final word. Truth does. And truth says:

Joy has arrived.

Acceptance echoes.

Hope reigns.

Peace sinks in.

Love abounds.

Guilt is destroyed.

Power grows.

Strength encompasses.

Comfort surrounds.

Jesus wins.

That is the truth Jesus knew—the truth He held onto in the face of His trauma. There would be victory in the end. Jesus would conquer the grave and rise from the dead. There was more to the story of trauma because trauma never gets the final word! The final word belongs to truth. It always has, and it always will.

Taking Inventory

What traumatic experiences has this chapter brought to the surface

of your heart? What would you scribble in your journal under the word
TRAUMA? What hurts and losses have you walked through, and how
have they shaped your life as a result? What could it look like to take
time and make space, inviting God to speak truth over the trauma in
your life? The mind doesn't just "forget" trauma. The body doesn't just
forget. The heart doesn't forget, either. Because forgetting is not the
answer to healing; in fact, it often makes things worse. The answer to
healing is not forgetting but transforming. Taking the old and making it new, in Jesus's mighty name. Replacing our trauma with truth.
Because truth must always get the final word.

Journaling Questions: 5-Minute Mental Health Checkup

- When you think about the word *trauma*, defined as a loss
  in your life or in the life of someone close to you, what
  experiences come to mind?

- How has trauma had an impact on your life physically,
  emotionally, relationally? Are there any other areas of your
  life that trauma has impacted?

- Take some time to practice exchanging trauma with truth
  by writing out a list of trauma you have experienced and
  then writing the truth that can offer new hope and perspective over that difficult experience. Set aside some time
  for prayer, asking God to speak truth over your trauma.
  Take some time to listen to what He might be saying to
  you.

- Set aside some time to practice mindfulness, allowing
  yourself to pay attention to your body, your heart, your
  relationships, and your experiences in the present.

- Write about what you feel and experience when you consider the trauma that Jesus faced in His own life.

PART 4

Physical Health
Getting Real with Your Body

Love the Lord your God...with all your strength.

LUKE 10:27

10

Back to the Basics

The Body-Mind Connection

My body was the *last* thing I was thinking about after my near-death experience. Which is ironic since it is the very thing that was almost taken from me. But I was not thinking about my body; I was thinking about my life. I was grateful to be alive, grateful to be able to come home to my children and husband, grateful for the new perspective that I was given—the reminder that this life is fleeting, and I had to make the most of every day. And in the wave of new gratitude, it is easy to dive into carpe diem mode without realizing that the body still remembers. The body still grieves. The body still needs to heal.

After my emergency surgery, my doctor gave me strict orders to rest and recover. Even though I had a seven-month-old baby at the time, I wasn't allowed to lift him. I had to reserve my strength for healing. So, that week, my mom and mother-in-law came to my side to help me care for my kids while I focused on recovery. What is strange about physical rest and recovery is that often you don't feel like you need it.

Your emotional and mental strength trick you into believing that you are fine—that *you are really okay*—all while your body is crying out for relief. I was completely exhausted from losing copious amounts of blood, sore all over, and severely cramping—but somehow, I still wanted to push through. Resting and recovering did not come naturally for me. I wanted to walk down the flight of stairs and check on my kids in the morning. I wanted to get dressed and resume my daily activity. I wanted to feel like I was adding value to my family by accomplishing something. But what I really needed to see and believe was that I was adding value just by taking care of myself. Just by resting.

I'll never forget when that revelation came to me just a couple of years later during the peak of an episode of depression and anxiety. I was in the thick of fatigue, overcome by the weight of depression and anxiety, and I remember one specific day my husband encouraged me to go upstairs and take a nap. I'm not naturally the kind of person who takes naps. I have a hard time shutting down midday and closing my eyes for a rest. But I was absolutely fatigued that day, so I took his advice. I remember tossing and turning in my bed that afternoon, feeling exhausted but all the while wrestling with guilt. One way you can recognize the voice of anxiety is that anxiety is an expert at filling you with guilt about everything—even about a 30-minute nap. My guilt told me I should be downstairs helping my husband, being there for my children, pushing through this exhaustion, and engaging with my family. But then, my God stepped in.

Let me preface this by saying how amusing it is when God uses something you absolutely have no interest in to get your attention. As I forced my eyes closed that day, God showed me a picture of a NASCAR race. Needless to say, that imagery caught my attention because it's something I would have never imagined on my own. I saw a red car zooming around and around and around the racetrack. And then I saw the red car pull over to the side, completely and utterly stopped in its tracks. Next, I saw a group of three men—the pit crew—surrounding that car and working diligently on changing out the tires, fueling it up, and checking the oil. Their job was to take care of the car while it rested so that it could resume the race.

That's when the Lord spoke to my heart in the most magnificent way, reminding me that HE was the pit crew, and I was that little red car. I needed to take the time to pull over and rest if I wanted to complete this race. I needed to refuel and recalibrate so that I could finish well. I needed to close my eyes, rest, and allow Him to take care of me physically in order for me to recover and resume what He had called me to do. Not only was rest a gift—it was vital. It was the only way that I could get back in the race. The race that He had called me to. I was reminded of the verse in Acts 20 when Paul affirms that "my only aim is to finish the race and complete the task the Lord Jesus has given me—the task of testifying to the good news of God's grace" (verse 24). I couldn't finish the race if I didn't allow God to heal my body while He healed my heart. I had permission—no, I had a job to do, and that job was to rest and recover. So, I closed my eyes and took the best nap of my life.

> Not only was rest a gift—it was vital.

Healing Is Holistic

We tend to talk about health in very compartmentalized ways:

Want spiritual health? Read your Bible.

Want mental health? Take an antidepressant.

Want emotional health? Be positive.

Want physical health? Eat your fruits and veggies.

But what if we began to see the impact that each one of these categories has on the others? What if we were to see healing as a holistic experience—an experience of our heart, soul, mind, and strength?

The mind-body connection helps us put proof to the idea that health is a holistic experience because it reminds us that everything is connected. Not only does our physical health impact our emotional and mental health, but it also goes the other way around. Research is rapidly increasing in this area, all pointing to the same thing: Everything is connected. One study showed that an increase of stress in participants led to diminished white blood cell function in response to both viral cells and cancer cells. Not only that, but "vaccination is less effective in those who are stressed, and wounds heal less readily in those who are stressed."[1]

If everything is connected, we have to begin seeing the importance of our physical actions and decisions with regard to the state of our overall mental and emotional health. Let's begin by looking at some of the physical habits that tend to have the biggest impact on our lives, beginning with sleep.

Sleep Hygiene

When you think of hygiene, you think of brushing your teeth, wearing deodorant, and taking regular showers. But this kind of hygiene has nothing to do with how you smell and everything to do with how you sleep. In fact, your sleep hygiene has an incredible impact on how well you sleep, which is important because how well you sleep has an incredible impact on how well you feel and function.[2]

My husband learned this the hard way. When he was in college, he decided to stay up all night to cram for an upcoming exam. It's a common practice for many college students, who naively assume that staying up late to study will result in better test scores the next day. He was especially concerned about his exam scores because he was looking ahead at applying to medical school, and he knew his scores had to stand out. When he got to his exam the next morning, he eagerly started writing down everything he had studied the night before. But within a few minutes, he couldn't help but notice how sleepy he was feeling, hypnotized by the rhythmic sound of the clock ticking in the quiet room. The next thing he remembers was waking up suddenly, with drool running down his face and the sudden realization that he had somehow slept through the entire test! There were minutes left on the clock, so he haphazardly answered as many questions as he could before time ran out. Needless to say, he totally bombed that exam.

Sleep is often an underestimated part to the equation of our overall health and mental well-being. But it's something we can't ignore because our body needs it to function properly. It impacts everything from our mood, to our judgment, to our ability to learn and retain information.[3] In addition, a lack of sleep impacts our physical health, including rates of cardiovascular disease, diabetes, obesity, metabolic syndrome, and mortality.[4]

While most sleep experts recommend a minimum of seven hours of sleep, many people are sleeping a lot less than that per night. The important thing to understand here is that your sleep hygiene impacts your sleep quality, which impacts your life. So, what exactly is sleep hygiene, and how do you incorporate that into your life? Sleep hygiene is a combination of healthy practices that encourage good sleep. A list of sleep hygiene practices would include some of the following:

- Avoiding caffeine close to bedtime

- Sleeping and waking at the same time every night

- Keeping your room cool and dark

- Limiting screen time before bed (the light from screens can arouse your body to wake mode)

- Limiting daytime naps to 30 minutes or less

- Following a similar bedtime routine each night

- Increasing your amount of sunshine during the day

- Exercising regularly during the day

If you are struggling with sleep, you might find yourself waking up multiple times throughout the night, waking up much earlier than you need to in the morning, or not being able to settle down and fall asleep at night. Putting some of these sleep hygiene strategies into effect can have a significant impact on your sleep.

I've always been really sensitive about my sleep hygiene, but especially after I got married because I realized that I don't have what I call "the gift of sleep," unlike my husband who can fall asleep in the middle of a college exam, a movie, or even a conversation. Some people have absolutely no problem with sleep, while others have to work for it.

Practicing a nightly routine and rhythm has been so helpful for me to make sure I get the sleep that my mind and body need. I have also noticed how much more vulnerable I am emotionally when I go through a season where I'm not sleeping well. I find myself getting overwhelmed, anxious, and upset much more quickly than I would have if I'd gotten a good night's rest. For me, a bedtime routine during seasons where I need to be deliberate about sleep looks like the following: dim lights, a hot shower or warm bath, relaxing music, aroma therapy (vanilla and lavender scents tend to help with relaxation), and taking some time to read and pray before bed. When it is finally time to sleep, I'm particular about having white noise to block out the rumbling of any traffic outside, and room-darkening blinds to keep the room dark and prepare my body for rest. I've been at this long enough that my body now associates those things with sleep. In fact, I was recently at a store when the smell of lavender wafted through the air as I walked by some candles, and I instantly got the feeling that it was time for bed!

Besides a nightly routine, it can also be helpful to keep a sleep diary, recording your sleep and wake times, particularly after you've tried a combination of different sleep hygiene methods to get an idea of what's working for you and what isn't. If you've been struggling with sleep for longer than two weeks, it's a good idea to reach out to your primary care doctor and see if they can discuss medication options with you or recommend an over-the-counter medication or natural sleep supplement like Melatonin (it's worked wonders for me during sleepless seasons).

But most importantly, when you're going through a season or a night of sleeplessness, don't panic! Anxiety arouses your entire system, sending an adrenaline rush throughout your body and giving it the message that it's time to get up and get going—which is the exact opposite of the feeling you're trying to produce. One way I've learned to counter anxiety about not sleeping when I want to sleep is by leaning into prayer during those hours of the night. The typical response would be to panic and think, *Oh no, why am I still awake? How am I going to function tomorrow? The hours are ticking by, and I'm running out of time to fall asleep!* But I've learned that response is not only unhelpful, it actually prevents me from relaxing and resting. It's counterproductive. So instead, I think, *Since I can't sleep right now, I'm going to use this time to connect with God. Maybe there's something He wants me to pray for, and I get an opportunity to have this pocket of time to focus on interceding for my family, my friends, and the world.*

> Lean into prayer during those dark hours of the night.

Instead of being filled with anxiety, I ask the Lord to fill me with His presence. I talk to Him about what I'm experiencing, what I'm feeling, and what I need. I ask Him to fill my mind and heart with His truth and with His peace. And usually, I end up drifting off to sleep somewhere in the process. I used to feel a little guilty about falling asleep during prayer until I read this beautiful quote from *Centering Prayer* by M. Basil Pennington, paralleling prayer to a child choosing to leave everything and jump into her father's arms:

> A father is delighted when his little one, leaving off her toys and friends, runs to him and climbs into his arms. As he holds his little one close to him, he cares little whether the child is looking around, her attention flitting from one thing to another, or just settling down to sleep. Essentially, the child is choosing to be with her father, confident of the love, the care, and the security that is hers in those

arms. Our prayer is much like that. We settle down in our Father's arms, in his loving hands. Our mind, our thoughts, our imagination may flit about here and there; we might even fall asleep; but essentially we are choosing for this time to remain intimately with our Father, giving ourselves to him, receiving his love and care, letting him enjoy us as he will. It is a very simple prayer. It is a very childlike prayer. It is a prayer that opens us out to all the delights of the kingdom.[5]

Falling asleep in Jesus's arms is the best way to fall asleep.

Physical Activity

There are two types of people in this world: those who love running and those who hate it. I am 100 percent in the latter category. To me, running is a form of voluntary torture. Why a person would put their body through such misery and call it "fun" is something my mind will never comprehend. I have always felt that way about it. I never understood my friends who go for "early morning runs" while on vacation. First of all, waking up *early* on vacation not only seems impractical, but a little insane. And then waking up early to torment my body? I'd rather skip vacation altogether.

But granted, not everyone feels that way about running. My friend Jessie is a cross-country runner. She goes on runs as her way of connecting to God. Running is her way of carving out the time and space she needs to focus inward on her breathing and upward on her God, the Giver of those breaths. It gives her a feeling of euphoria, decreases her anxiety, and helps her stay centered. And even though I'll never totally grasp that perspective, there is no denying the power of physical activity on our emotional and mental health. Our bodies impact every other part of our being.

Whether you are a runner or not, it is important to understand how intertwined our emotional, mental, spiritual, and physical health are. Impacting one area ultimately impacts the others. In fact, research proves this again and again. One study showed a significant decrease in clinical depression in a group of people who engaged in weekly physical activity (20 to 40-minute walks three times a week for six weeks) versus the control group who did not engage in physical activity. Physical activity clearly decreased both the emotional and psychosomatic symptoms of depression, but not only that, the results of some exercise-focused studies showed a decrease in depression and anxiety symptoms for up to 12 months later.[6] That's an entire year later, still benefiting from the mental benefits of walking! It makes me wonder why we seem to talk about the benefits of physical activity so infrequently in the conversation of overall mental and emotional health.

As a thirty-something-year-old parent of three children (that sounds better than saying late thirties), I'm a generally active person by default, but only because chasing three kids around requires me to move my body. But I'm not going to pretend I've prioritized my physical activity. In fact, I've realized over the past year just how little I've put into this important area. As a counselor, my tendency is to spotlight emotional and mental health. But as I'm nearing age 40, I'm recognizing my need to focus on the strength and health and well-being of my body. I'm starting to ache in places I've never ached before, and I'm noticing muscles begin to weaken and atrophy because, frankly, I don't use them anymore. My lower back pain got so bad after having three children that I found myself in physical therapy last year. The conclusion? My core was weak, and it was impacting my posture and spine alignment.

As easy as it might be to file this away as an isolated incident, it's important to remember that everything is connected. Healing is holistic. When my back aches, I can't be as active as I want to be. When my back aches, my body is sending pain messages to my brain, which then tells my body to slow down. When I'm forced to slow down, I lose motivation. When I lose motivation, I begin to feel apathetic. It's all connected because physical health ultimately impacts all the other moving pieces.

So, I've been taking the next steps to prioritize my physical activity. Even though I despise running, I've learned that I absolutely love walking. When I travel for a speaking engagement, John and I always make it a point to explore the city we're visiting. Our most recent trip to New Orleans found us walking a minimum of seven miles a day. I realized how much I enjoy walking and how easy it comes for me, so when we got home, I bought myself a low-cost bracelet pedometer that I've been wearing every day with the goal of 10,000 steps per day. Not only that, but I've found that I can also tolerate jogging. I had to start somewhere, and I had to find something that works for me that I could integrate into my schedule easily and simply. When it's simple, you're more likely to succeed in doing it. The key is to take inventory of your physical activity and ask yourself how it is impacting your overall health. What changes can you make to take the next step in this important area of your life?

Nutritional Health

Recently, I went to a gas station to fill my car with fuel, but I was a little distracted with thoughts buzzing around my mind about an upcoming project that day. In my brain fog, I accidentally grabbed the wrong gas dispenser and was about to fill my car with diesel fuel (the kind those big semitrucks use). Thankfully, I snapped back to reality just in time and noticed because the wrong fuel would have completely jacked up my car. Though it looks and smells the same as regular gasoline, diesel fuel would have clogged up my fuel lines and could have caused permanent damage to my engine.

What we put in our car really matters. But more importantly, what we put into our body really matters. It might all look and smell similar, but some foods have the power to heal our physical body while others have the power to damage it. Not only does food impact our body but, because everything is interrelated, it has the power to impact everything else. There is science behind our food and its connection to our mood. In fact, because of the close relationship between our brain and digestive system, the gastrointestinal tract has often been called our "second brain." When we fill our bodies with healthy foods, the good bacteria in our gastrointestinal tract increase and impact the production of neurotransmitters (the feel-good chemicals that we talked about earlier). The more neurotransmitters our body is producing, the better we feel. On the other hand, foods that cause inflammation decrease the production of neurotransmitters.[7] Our food has a great impact on our mood. "While the determining factors of mental health are complex, increasing evidence indicates a strong association between a poor diet and the exacerbation of mood disorders, including anxiety and depression, as well as other neuropsychiatric conditions."[8] Not only that, but the increase of research in this field has led to the coining of the new term "nutritional psychiatry," referring to the way our diet impacts our mental and emotional health.

In one study, foods that caused an increase in inflammation and an overall higher risk of developing depression were sugar-sweetened soft drinks, refined grains, red meat, diet soft drinks, and margarine. Foods with a low inflammatory response included wine, coffee, olive oil, green leafy and yellow vegetables.[9] In fact, what some call the Mediterranean diet (rich in fish, legumes, olive oil, and whole grains) has been linked to a lower prevalence of depression.[10]

There is so much more that could be said on this topic far beyond the scope of this section. In fact, entire books have been written on the connection of food and mood. There is new and emerging research about the role of things such as probiotics and their value for increasing the good bacteria, which ultimately impacts our mood and our overall well-being. My goal in this short portion of the book isn't to offer a plan or even a solution, but rather to offer perspective and to make a case for the vital role our nutrition plays in our health physically, mentally, and emotionally.

Taking Inventory

According to God's Word, our bodies are a temple of the Holy

Spirit (1 Corinthians 6:19). They are the living, breathing temple where God makes His home. If that's the case, then it is up to us to make sure we're giving our body the rest it needs to function properly, strengthening it with physical activity and fueling our body with foods that are going to move us toward health and functioning to the best of our ability. Everything is connected, and when we make a shift in one area, it begins to impact all the others.

Journaling Questions: 5-Minute Physical Checkup

- On a scale of 1 (being the worst) to 10 (being the best), how would I rate the quality of my sleep in the past two weeks? What is one way I can begin to make a change to focus on better sleep?

- On a scale of 1 (being the worst) to 10 (being the best), how would I rate the quality of my physical activity in the past two weeks? What is one way I can begin to make a change to focus on increased physical activity?

- On a scale of 1 (being the worst) to 10 (being the best), how would I rate the quality of my nutrition the past two weeks? What is one way I can begin to make a change to focus on better nutrition?

- In what ways have I noticed the impact of sleep, physical activity, and nutrition on my overall health and well-being—emotionally, physically, and mentally?

11

Stop Living on Empty

The Art of Self-Care

I've never been good at filling up my gas tank in time. I'm an effi-
cient person, and I don't like to take the extra time to do things if I
don't absolutely have to. But sometimes I take that to the extreme. I
remember one day, on the way to a ministry event, I noticed my gas
light was signaling it was time to fill up. But calculating my minutes
like I often do, I didn't want to waste time filling up before the event in
order use every possible moment to pour into the people at the event.
So, I decided to wait until after the event was over.

The only problem was, after the event, I realized there was no gas
station nearby. I drove around for a while, noticing my gas meter was
now slowly falling *under* the E mark. I was past empty and probably
running on fumes. I went into hypervigilant mode, glancing every
which way for a place to fuel up. To my surprise and thanks to God's
kindness, I saw a gas station at the bottom of the hill after I turned the

next corner. It was close enough, and there was a good chance I could make it there before I ran out of gas. But literally, about 100 feet from the gas station, my car engine began to sputter. And then, the engine shut down. I was totally out of gas.

At this point, it was either stop the car and get out and push, or let it keep coasting down the hill. So, I put my car in neutral and hoped for the best. This is what I call a modern-day miracle, my friends, because my car literally coasted down the hill and into the gas station parking lot, stopping just a few feet from the only available gas pump. *Thank You, Jesus!* Talk about a close call! I'm not sure why, but I never imagined it was possible to actually run out of gas until it happened. Let this be a public service announcement to all of you unbelievers out there: Running out of gas is a real thing. There is a limited supply of fuel, even though you can't see it. That little gas meter actually knows what it's doing. It's telling the truth! Ever since that close call, I have never let my car get to less than a quarter tank of gas before I fill up. I recognize when I'm nearing *E* long before I get there.

Empty Looks Like This

By God's grace, He has allowed me to have the same vision for my personal health as well. After experiencing some extremely close calls with my near-death experience, as well as my struggles with depression and anxiety, I've learned that I have to be proactive with my personal health rather than reactive.

I can't *wait* until I'm emotionally and physically empty before I take seriously the need to fill up. I have to be deliberate and intentional about making sure I'm filled up long before I get to a place of spiritual, emotional, mental, and physical emptiness. I've got to watch my meter by being in tune to what I need and when I need it. Because it's possible to get to empty and find ourselves completely drained and quickly shutting down.

While we don't have a literal meter that tells us when we're nearing empty, it's important for us to be in tune with our bodies and our emotions in order to know when we're starting to run low on fuel. I know I'm getting close to empty when these things start to happen:

- I find myself getting irritable or impatient with my husband and kids.

- I feel drained and physically tired throughout the day (even before I've done anything).

- I find myself snacking on junk food instead of taking the time to fill up in a nutritious way.

- I'm running low on motivation to get things done that I need to do.

- I want to "veg" and zone out more often than I want to do something stimulating.

- I'm running low on creativity and inspiration.

- I start feeling increased stress or anxiety about things that normally wouldn't bother me.

Some other signs to be on the lookout for when you might be nearing empty:

- Increased stress and frustration with work, people, or responsibilities

- Physical symptoms such as headaches or chronic fatigue

- Lacking in energy to get things done that you need to do

- Difficulty concentrating, lack of sustained mental energy, or an increase in forgetfulness

- Feelings of cynicism, bitterness, or resentment with the people around you

- A lack of accomplishment or a feeling of ineffectiveness when you try to get something done

- Increased feelings of anxiety and depression or a heightened sense of worry

> **The one and only ingredient you need for burnout is this: the false notion that you can do it all.**

It's important to understand the signs of what it looks like for *you* to be nearing empty. In counseling and psychology, we often refer to this experience as "burnout." And it can happen to anyone, anywhere, at any age, and anytime. The one and only ingredient you need for burnout is this: the false notion that you can do it all.

The Myth of *Doing It All*

How do you do it all?

I get that question on a regular basis. From the outside looking in, my life looks full. And in many ways, it is. I'm a wife, a homeschooling mom of three kids under 10, a blogger, author, podcaster, and licensed counselor. Add to that I'm a daughter, a granddaughter, and a friend. The energy and effort it takes to manage all those different yet important roles is something I'm acutely aware of. Which is why my response to the above question always comes in the form of five secret words: *I don't do it all.*

That's the honest truth. Because I have learned over the years, thanks to a lot of trial and error, that I *can't* do it all and expect to survive. I can't do it *all*, but I *can* do a few things well. And that has always been my mantra. In order to stick to a few significant things, I've had to get really good at repeating one simple word: *no.*

Over the past few years, *no* has become one of the most essential words in my vocabulary. It is the word that I use as a surgeon uses his scalpel, cutting out all the unnecessary and even harmful things in my life. *No* keeps out the excess, allowing me to focus in on the few things God has called me to. But for most people, *no* isn't a word that comes naturally. The cultural tendency is to say yes, so much yes—until we find ourselves burned out and run down. We live in a culture that is all about productivity and accomplishment. We use phrases like "climbing the ladder" and "the sky is the limit" without ever realizing that even climbers need to rest and that we are bound by physical and emotional limits. We have limits, and there's absolutely no shame in acknowledging that. We all have a limited supply of physical, emotional, and mental fuel, and if we are not aware of it, it will run out. We'll find ourselves living on empty, and eventually, not living at all. *No* is my magic word because I see it as a declaration of my limitations. It's the proof that I can't do it all. It's a reminder of my humanity and a reality check that reminds me that I am not invincible.

> I use the word *no* as a surgeon uses his scalpel, cutting out all the unnecessary and even harmful things in my life.

People often feel bad about saying no. In a way, they would rather not face their limits, so instead of saying no, they say yes. But it's important to realize that the word *yes* actually has *no* built into it. It is just a *no* you're not in control of. Because every time you say yes to something, you are automatically saying no to something else, but passively, without taking consideration of the outcome.

- *Yes* to an unscheduled phone call with a client is an automatic *no* to evening family time.

- *Yes* to an extra ministry opportunity is an automatic *no* to an opportunity for rest.

- *Yes* to an extra sporting activity in the evening is an automatic *no* to gathering as a family for dinner.

- *Yes* to a few more hours of work is an automatic *no* to a few extra hours of quality time with my spouse.

- *Yes* to that early morning friendly gathering is an automatic *no* to the time I reserved for the extra sleep my body needs.

Every *yes* comes at a cost. I wonder if we'd be so scared of *no* if we fully realized that every *yes* has an automatic *no* built into it. My eyes have been opened over the years to the reality that I need to build boundaries around my life by the things I say yes and no to. With every no, I am building a fence around my life, my family, and my ministry that keeps the good things in and the harmful things out. With every no, I am allowing God to take away the excess and help me focus on the things that really matter—the things He's called me to do in my family and for His kingdom. With every no, I am reserving my emotional, mental, and physical fuel for the things that really matter the most.

> We can't do it all because we weren't made to do it all.

Like I said before, this has come with a lot of trial and error on my part. If you'll remember earlier in the book, I shared with you the value statements that I've carried over the years, believing that "doing" was where my value came from. The more I did, the better I felt, and vice versa. One of the gifts God has given me through the dark valleys of depression and anxiety is learning to see tangibly that I have limits. Limits to what I can do. Limits to what I can accomplish. Limits that came in the form of my body literally "stopping," unable to perform or accomplish under the weight of depression. Limits that remind me that I can't do it all because I wasn't made to do it all.

No creates margin. It makes space in our lives that we would not otherwise have. Space to breathe. Space to connect. Space to listen. Space to stop and take inventory of how healthy we are; it gives us space to heal. Space to fill up and be refreshed. This looks different for everyone because you have to find your own pace as well as your own space, but I wanted to share how this practically plays out in my personal life and give you some examples.

No to My Job

- I make it a point to only tackle one big project at a time.

That usually looks like dedicating a specific season to only record podcasts, or only work on book writing, or only curate blog posts.

- No matter how much work I have, Sundays are always reserved for rest, family, and Sabbath.

- I limit my speaking engagements to a certain number per month and do not exceed that number no matter how many opportunities come up.

- I commit to taking off from traveling from Thanksgiving to New Year's to make sure I'm prioritizing the things that matter during the holiday season.

No in My Home

- As parents, John and I say no to doing it all around the house! John and I have worked on teaching our children how to do chores and be responsible for their portion of things around the house such as cleaning and laundry so that we can maximize our quality time as a family.

- I reserve a portion of my budget to hire help with deep cleaning once a month and use that time for ministry and family instead.

- Since I'm usually the primary caregiver during the day, I've asked my husband to take over the bedtime routine so I can have that time to work out, meet with a friend, read a book, or do what I need to do to at the end of each day to refresh and recharge with time away from the kids.

No to My Activities

- We limit the kids to one activity per season so that our schedule isn't filled with running around from place to place with drop-offs and pickups.

- We say no to extra ministry commitments. A lot of ministry opportunities come up through the year, and they are all so good and important. But we have focused on the few things God has called us to and say no to anything else.

- We commit to having at least five family dinners together each week, so extra activities that would impede on that commitment always go in the *no* category.

- When it comes to weekends, we make it a point to have just one social gathering per weekend with friends and say no to any additional activities.

In all of these scenarios, *no* is the magic word because it helps us make room for the things that really matter and invest in doing a few things well.

Go, Go, Go, Go…STOP!

My four-year-old has a favorite construction vehicles book that shows a world in which there is no "stop." Everyone is just going, going, going, and life begins to get chaotic. Until one day, STOP rolls into town and shows them the importance of having GO and STOP work together in unison.

There's a lot of life lessons you can learn from a children's board book because we live in such a go, go, go world that often we don't stop until we're forced to. We don't stop until life gets chaotic. We don't stop until we burn out. But being a healthy person means that we recognize our limits long before we hit them.

Mike's Story

You don't expect to see a powerful CEO in a crisp, blue blazer, sitting in a counseling office. He doesn't fit the mold of the stereotypical client you might imagine, who comes in asking for help. Mike may have not fit the stereotype, but he definitely fit the description of burnout. He came into counseling after putting it off for quite some time because ironically, he was too busy. He was a husband and father of two teenagers. He was the CEO of a major multimillion-dollar company. Add to that, he was an elder at his church and actively involved in ministry. But Mike was on the verge of what he called a "mental breakdown." The stress of his job was building up to the point where he was working more and more and sleeping less and less. The more he worked, the less he slept, and the more stressed he became. The stress began accumulating and impacting his relationship with his wife, building more tension and pressure underneath the surface. Not only that, but then there were the demands of his aging parents, his commitment to his church, and his conviction to be there for his two daughters. All of this was starting to impact his personal health, and Mike found himself battling physical symptoms as well as emotional symptoms of anxiety, hopelessness, and despair.

"I don't know what's wrong with me," Mike told me, his eyes welling up with tears. "I just can't seem to juggle it all..."

And there, beneath his desperate words, I found the lie that Mike and so many of us tell ourselves. The lie that convinces us that somehow we are supposed to do it all. The lie that fools us into believing that we have unlimited resources, that we should do all things and be all things to all people.

Looking back at his history, Mike was a firstborn son in a blue-collar family. His dad worked long and hard hours, and Mike grew up believing that a dad's job was to provide at all costs, even at the cost of detachment from his family. Not only that, but Mike was the older brother to a set of twins that came next. He spent a lot of his childhood filling in the gaps and helping his mom when his dad wasn't available. He learned quickly that he was responsible for "holding the family together" and that saying yes was not optional. He had to be all things to all people, or life would fall apart. He took that mentality with him after leaving home, always being willing to take on one too many roles and wear one too many hats. He was the provider, the caregiver, the motivator, the peacemaker, and the listening ear. If he didn't take care of it, who would?

Mike believed the lie that *he* was responsible for taking care of everything and everyone around him. He had to say yes, or life would fall apart. And with that theme, he continued saying yes when everything inside of him cried out no. Yes to increased hours at work. Yes to more meetings. Yes to heading up another ministry at church. Yes to his aging parents' needs and desires. Yes to his children's sporting events. Yes to the men's pancake breakfast at church. Yes to that after-hours business dinner. Yes to that extended work conference. Until one day, his body could take it no more. That's the day Mike, in his crisp, blue blazer, came to see me. Because something needed to change.

The Roots of Yes

For most of us, it's not as simple as just starting to say no more and yes less. Like Mike, we all have an underlying motivation for the reason we say yes to too many things, the reason we like to stay busy, the reason we go, go, go, go...before we're forced to stop. For some people like Mike, it is the underlying false assumption of responsibility—that we need to be all things to all people. For others like me, it's the underlying false value statement that *I am what I do*. For others still, it is the fear of missing out, desperately wanting to be involved and engaged in what everyone else is doing. For others yet, it is the fear of being still, left to face their own thoughts and struggles because it's easier to stay busy than it is to stop and heal. We have to get to the bottom of the reason we say yes in order to allow yes and no to live in unison.

For Mike, this meant coming to the realization that he is not responsible for how everyone else feels and what everyone else needs. He had to learn to let go, say no, and trust that the God who held all things together would continue holding all things together even when Mike no longer could. By saying no, he was releasing himself from the burdens and responsibility he was carrying that were never meant for him, and instead, casting them on the Lord, believing that God would sustain him like He promises in His Word (Psalm 55:22). He did not have to be all things to all people because that was God's job.

It sounds simple, but the roots of our yeses can run so deep that we often fail to recognize them until we find ourselves depleted and burned out. When Mike began recognizing the underlying motivation behind his yes, he was able to face it in practical ways. He was able to see that he didn't have to say yes to those extra hours at work because the company didn't rise and fall on his extra hours. He was able to realize that he didn't have to say yes to every ministry opportunity that was requested of him because there were others who were capable of carrying the responsibility. He was able to see that in saying yes to coworkers, friends, and the never-ending list of requests, he was actually saying no to his peace, his health, and his emotional and spiritual well-being. He realized the irony that if he was burned out and depleted, he was actually of no use to the people around him. Because you can't give to others what you don't have yourself.

> We have to get to the bottom of the reason we say yes in order to allow yes and no to live in unison.

Time to Fill Up

Let me ask you this important question: What fills you up? I wonder if you know the answer to that question, or if it's something you need to take the time to think through. The answer to this question changes everything because it points you in the direction of taking care of yourself. When you hear the word *self-care*, what's your internal reaction? Many Christians tend to have an adverse reaction to the word *self-care*. There's an underlying false (and, might I add, dangerous) belief that the word *self-care* is somehow selfish because it's focused on self. It's an assumption that leads to the false notion that to focus on caring for yourself means to stop focusing on God and others. But the two are not mutually exclusive. In fact, Jesus Himself modeled the principles of self-care in how He lived His life.

I always point to the scripture that reminds us to "love your neighbor as yourself" (Matthew 22:39). Jesus could have just as easily commanded us to love our neighbor *more* than we love ourselves, but He didn't. He

> When we stop caring for ourselves we become empty. Ironically, empty people are the most self-centered and self-absorbed of all.

could have encouraged us to "love your neighbor *not* yourself," but He didn't say that either. He chose that specific set of words for a specific reason. I wonder if it's because He knew that loving God and loving others weren't mutually exclusive with loving ourselves. I wonder if it's because He knew that self-loathing and self-neglect were just as harmful as vanity and self-centeredness. When we stop caring for ourselves, we become empty. Ironically, empty people are the most self-centered and self-absorbed of all. Think about the time you felt the emptiest. For me, in those moments of empty, all I could think about was how bad I felt and how empty I was. I was so drained that I was unable to look up at God or out at the needs of others. Empty people lose their joy, their empathy, and their motivation to keep on giving. By not caring for ourselves, we become self-focused—the very thing we were trying to avoid in the first place.

Jesus knew the importance of fueling up long before He got to empty. He knew that in order to do the work that God had called Him to do, He had to take the time to care for Himself physically, emotionally, mentally, and spiritually. He had to fill up. And He modeled that to us in three specific ways:

1. *He surrounded Himself with the right people.* Jesus was so good at cultivating community. He knew the value of surrounding Himself with the right people on the journey of life. He hand-selected the people who would walk by His side in the give-and-take of true friendship. They did ministry together, but they also had fun together. They went to weddings, they ate meals together, they visited friends together, and they simply enjoyed each other's company. These are the kind of

friendships that are both filling and fulfilling. We can learn so much from the idea of seeing our friendships and community as a crucial part of keeping ourselves healthy and filled up. This is such a practical part to the picture of self-care. Jesus didn't haphazardly choose His people; He prayerfully chose His people. Scripture tells us that He had spent an entire night in prayer before choosing who would be His disciples the next morning (Luke 6:12-13). What type of people are you surrounding yourself with, and are they people who help to fill you up, or do they wear you down? Taking care of yourself means being deliberate about who you allow to surround you.

2. *He took time to rest and recharge.* Some of my favorite passages in Scripture are when Jesus stops to take a rest. The idea of Jesus sleeping makes me feel deeply the importance of rest and recharging in my own life. In a way, it's actually arrogant for me to think I don't need it, when God Himself took the time to prioritize it. Mark 4:35-40 tells of one such story when Jesus had just finished a significant day of ministry. There were still crowds, and there were still needs to be met, but even so, Jesus recognized His own needs and the need of His disciples for rest. "Let's go over to the other side," He told them. And they took the boat to the other side of the lake for a little peace and quiet. In fact, Jesus climbed in the boat, went down to the stern, and fell asleep on a cushion, sleeping right through a big storm until His disciples woke Him up to make it stop (Mark 4:38)! He made time to rest. But not only that, He encouraged His disciples to do the same. A few chapters later, we see Jesus urging His disciples to come away with Him to eat, to rest, and to recharge (Mark 6:31-32). It makes me smile to think of Jesus in this way, so in tune to His own needs, yet so in tune to the needs of others.

3. *He loaded up on prayer.* Jesus knew that self-care wasn't complete until He allowed Himself to be filled up by connecting with the Father. He made time for prayer, unplugging from everything and everyone else to plug in to God. Luke 5:16 finds Him withdrawing to "lonely places" to pray. A few chapters later, we see Jesus committing an entire

evening to prayer, spending the whole night connecting with God (Luke 6:12). Talk about a time of filling up! Another time, we see Jesus waking up while it was still dark, before the sun was even out, just to make sure to get that time alone to pray (Mark 1:35). I don't know about you, but it's been a while since I spent an entire night in prayer. It's even hard for me to wake up early or stay up a little later to pray. But I wonder how much I'm robbing myself of getting "filled up" because of the lack of prayer in my life. Sure, I pray before meals, when I wake up in the morning, and usually before I go to bed. But I have a disturbing tendency to see prayer as the thing to "check off my list" rather than my real, true, desperate need to be filled up. Jesus knew the importance of prayer as His lifeline to the Father. Scripture is full of these examples! It challenges me to take inventory of my own heart and my own tendency to "fill up" on things that don't really fill me up. As I reflect on my own life, I wonder if maybe getting filled up well means putting that book down to pray. Or turning off that Netflix show I've been binge watching this week to pray. Or giving up a few moments of sleep to wake up early and pray. Or shutting off my Instagram scroll for a day to pray. Not because I have to check it off my to-do list, but because, just like Jesus, *I need it to survive.*

Please, please, please don't get me wrong here, I am *all about* taking time to fill up by watching a movie, taking a nap, or reading a good book. Sometimes, self-care means lounging in my hammock and staring up at the sky, window-shopping at Target, grabbing my journal and heading to my favorite coffee shop, or asking my husband for a back rub. Those things are all necessary and enjoyable. But I also know that those things can only take me so far. Ultimately, I need to be emptied of myself in order to be filled up with Him.

I'm asking God to change my heart in this important area of self-care. To see His presence in my life and His filling of my heart as a desperate need, rather than just a bonus. And I wonder if maybe, just maybe, you need to ask God for the same.

Taking Inventory

I don't know where you fall on the meter of feeling empty right now. Maybe you're feeling filled to the brim, bubbling with energy, and bursting with motivation. Maybe you're feeling completely drained and depleted, wondering where you'll get strength for tomorrow. But if you're anything like me, you find that meter oscillating from *full* to almost *empty* on a regular basis. You resonate with both sides of the spectrum. That's why it's important to understand that the need to be filled is not a once-and-done experience; it's part of our everyday process. It's something we need to take inventory of at the end or the beginning of each and every new day. How full are you feeling, and more importantly, what does it look like to *take* time to get filled up? The answer to that question takes you one step closer to becoming healthy from the inside out.

Journaling Questions: 5-Minute Physical Checkup

- Am I usually a yes person or a no person?

- What are the "roots" of my yes? In other words, why do I have a hard time saying no? What are some areas in my life that I need to practice saying no?

- When I think of the term *self-care*, what is my internal reaction and why?

- On a scale of feeling FULL (10) to EMPTY (0), what number am I currently?

- What are some personal signs that I exhibit when I am nearing empty?

- When it comes to self-care, take some time to list out specific ways you can be deliberate about filling up with community, with rest, and with prayer.

12

Time Doesn't Heal All Wounds

One Year from Today

Time heals all wounds."

Whoever coined that phrase must have never experienced any kind of trauma or loss. Time alone might heal small wounds, but it doesn't heal all wounds.

Sure, if all you have is a "paper cut" on your heart, a little passing of time will get you to a better place. But if you have a festering wound—a broken heart, a tragic loss, a traumatic experience, shattered trust, a painful childhood—please, don't tell me that time will heal all wounds. Because it can't.

Time alone doesn't have that kind of power.

Simply putting space between you and a festering wound doesn't make it go away. In fact, it may get even more infected with the passing of time. You have to give it attention and tender care for healing to happen. You have to be intentional. You have to go backward and deal with the wound before you can move forward into healing.

One thing I see that happens so often on an emotional level is that people ignore significant heart and soul wounds, expecting them to heal with time. But they only get worse and worse along the way. Because time doesn't have the power to heal all wounds.

> A year from now, you won't be any healthier than you are today unless you choose to be.

A year from now, 365 days will have passed. But you won't be any healthier than you are today unless you choose to be. Because time alone can't get you there. You have to learn to live intentionally, partnering with God in the process of healing. You have to be purposeful and deliberate. You have to be willing and prepared to acknowledge the past, understand the past, and then deal with the past hand in hand with Jesus. Because time can't heal all wounds. Only Jesus can.

Walking with a Limp

We've got to be careful never to think the word *healing* means perfection. God's Word tells us that because of Jesus's wounds and His experience on the cross, our souls can be healed once and for all (Isaiah 53:5). We don't have to fear condemnation, punishment, or death because Jesus has victory over it all in the end. We are more than conquerors because of the fact that nothing in this world, not even death, can separate us from God's love (Romans 8:31-39). We can have full confidence in that fact while still acknowledging that in this world we can't reach perfection. In this world, there will be pain and heartache. In this world, there will be temptation. In this world, there will be trouble (John 16:33). In this world, we will have scars. In this world, we may find ourselves walking with a limp.

There are few sermons that stick with you for a lifetime, but this one did. I've never been able to shake it from my mind, and I never want to. In this gut-wrenching message, Jon Courson tells the tragic story of how he lost his first wife, and then years later, his 16-year-old daughter—both in tragic car accidents. In an instant, trauma became a part of his life, scribbling with its awful strokes all over the page of his story. In an instant, his heart was overtaken by searing pain. Not just once, but twice.

How does a person recover from that kind of experience? Is it even possible to use the word *healing* in the context of such severe and life-altering pain? What about the couple who suddenly and unexpectedly lost their five-year-old daughter days before Christmas? Or the woman who became a widow at age 25 after her husband suddenly dropped dead, and was left with three kids under age three to raise alone? What about the former drug addict who looks at his arm and sees scar after scar from where the needles pierced his skin, reminding him of the scars he holds inside? What about the grown man who carries the wounds of his childhood, shamed and abused at the hands of the father who was supposed to love him? What about the couple who glance at one another with pain as they recall the graphic suicide of their teenage son and wonder what they could have done differently? What about the man who was falsely accused, ripped away from his family and thrown in prison, and left alone to suffer through the greatest injustice of his life? What about the missionary's young daughter, raped and assaulted at the international boarding school that was meant to keep her safe from harm? What about the young couple, desperately longing for children, hearing the tragic news at 26 weeks that their baby had died in the womb?

These aren't just stories on a page. These are lives. Real lives. Lives of people I personally know and deeply love. Lives that carry the strokes of trauma and pain and loss and heartbreak written all over their stories. Is healing even possible for them? Can we be so naive as to think that time can heal such aching wounds? In the sermon by Jon Courson, he goes on to explain that God opened his eyes to two starkly different passages in Scripture—both involving people who needed healing.[1]

The first is the story of the man at the pool of Bethesda. He had suffered from a severe condition that kept him paralyzed and unable to move for 38 years (John 5:1-15). But in an instant, Jesus healed him, and immediately he was able to get up and walk. A little while later, when the man was confronted by a group of Jews asking who healed him, his response was simply, "I don't know. I don't know who healed me." He was healed in an instant, but he did not know the One who healed him.

The next story is the story of Jacob. Jacob is a man who went through severe trauma as well, having experienced family dysfunction and conflict that left him running for his life. He endured heartbreak and became the victim of deceit, just as he himself had once deceived. But one unexpectedly momentous night, Jacob came face-to-face with the Great Healer. He saw God face-to-face, and he wrestled with Him until God gave him a blessing. After that experience, Jacob was injured, and from that point on he walked with a limp (Genesis 32:31-32). Although he was blessed, he never *fully* recovered. But in his trauma, tragedy, and heartbreak, he came face-to-face with God. He *knew* God, yet he walked with a limp. I wonder if every step he took, every limping journey, every hardship from that day on reminded him of his need for God? Reminded him of his dependence on God? One man was made perfectly well but forgot Jesus. The other man walked with a limp, but always remembered his God.

If you asked me to choose between a life of perfection where I don't know Jesus or a life with a limp but intimacy with my Savior, I would choose the limp *every single time*. In fact, I see my own limp on the regular. I see the scars of depression and anxiety, I feel the heartbreak and loss of the baby I won't get to meet until heaven, I experience the uncertainty and fear that comes with almost losing my life. But I also see hope. I have hope that because of this limp, I get to lean on Jesus more than I ever would without it. I have hope in knowing that through my pain, struggles, and hardships, I've gotten to know my Father in a way I would have otherwise never known Him. I have hope in believing that just as I have gotten to know Jesus through the pain of my suffering, I also get to know Him in the power of His resurrection. "I want to know Christ—yes, to know the power of his resurrection and participation in his sufferings, becoming like him in his death, and so, somehow, attaining to the resurrection from the dead" (Philippians 3:10-11). I

> With my pain comes His power.

may not get to rewrite my story, but I have hope in knowing that, because of Jesus, I get to decide how it ends. Because with my pain comes His power.

Hope Has the Last Word

Here's what we desperately need to understand: Healing doesn't mean perfection. Healing doesn't mean that we can erase the pain of our past. Healing doesn't mean that we get to rewrite our experiences and choose a different story. But what we have the power to choose is how the story ends. What we have is the ability to look at our scars and remember Jesus—the God who chose to carry scars Himself. Scars that remind us that in this world we will have trouble, but that there is One who has overcome this world, and His name is Jesus (John 16:33). This world is not our final destination, and we can't be surprised by the pain we experience here. And while we don't have the power to undo our experiences, we have the power to overcome our experiences by not allowing them to have the final word in the stories we are writing for ourselves. Only Jesus gets the final word. And the final word for each of us is *hope*.

Hope that you can be restored (1 Peter 5:10).

Hope that you can endure (1 Thessalonians 1:3).

Hope that you can be made strong (Isaiah 40:31).

Hope that God has a plan (Jeremiah 29:11).

Hope that you are not forgotten (Psalm 9:18).

Hope that God will sustain you (Psalm 3:5).

Hope that you will be saved (Romans 8:24).

Hope that you can have peace (Romans 15:13).
Hope that all of this will be used for good (Romans 8:28).
Hope that there is a better life that's eternal (Titus 1:1-2).
Hope that Jesus gets the final word in your story and in mine (Philippians 1:6).

Healing Looks Like This

We often expect the process of healing to look like a one-way trek up the side of a mountain, getting higher and higher with each step. We assume that true healing means we just get better and better each day. No turning back, right? The problem with that belief is it's not only impossible, it's also unrealistic. By holding on to the belief that healing means we only get better and better with each step, we set ourselves up for failure and disappointment when it doesn't go as planned.

True healing isn't linear. It's less like a trek up the side of a mountain and more like a spiral. Sometimes healing looks more like taking two steps forward and one step back. We may have to go backwards sometimes, knowing that we're getting stronger and healthier each time through. We don't have to be afraid when we find ourselves paused for a while, or even backtracking every now and again, because we know that we're just gaining strength and perspective to be able to go even farther the next few steps.

365 Days from Today: Stages of Change

Becoming healthy doesn't just happen with time; it happens with intention. You can even *want* to move toward health, but wanting alone isn't enough to get you there. Time is going to pass for you and me both, and only you get to decide where you will be 365 days from today. You can either be in the same place as you are today, or you can be closer to healthy. In fact, because change is such an intentional process, it's something that can actually be mapped out. In counseling, I often refer to the five stages of change to give people an idea of what this looks like practically—of the difference between just wanting something and moving intentionally toward it.

Stage 1: Precontemplation—The first stage of change is when something worth changing is finally on your radar. Maybe you go to the doctor, and she's concerned with your BMI or blood pressure. Or maybe you finished reading a book about becoming healthy, and you're starting to wonder if there's something you need to work on. Maybe you were close to losing something or someone you love, and now it has got you thinking. Either way, the first stage of change is precontemplation, meaning you haven't thought too much about change, but now it's at least on your radar. You aren't serious about change at this point, but something has caused you to at least consider that there may be areas in your life that could benefit from a change.

Stage 2: Contemplation—The second stage of change is when you finally start thinking through what it would look like to do things differently. You weigh the pros and cons of changing, and the scale starts tipping in the direction of change. At this point, maybe you're sick and tired of dealing with anxiety on a regular basis, and you've finally decided it's time to try to get help. Maybe you get on the scale, and it's so far from your ideal healthy weight that you decide it's finally time to do something about it. At this point in the stages of change, the motivation is beginning to grow. You see the problem more clearly than you ever have before. You've moved from considering change to wanting change.

Stage 3: Preparation—This is the stage when the process of change practically begins. You go from wanting something to getting ready for it. This would be the stage where you map out a plan of how you are going to get from point A to point B. If you're trying to lose weight, for example, this would be the stage when you start educating yourself about nutrition and exercise, research some weight-loss apps, or plan out your weekly menu of healthy meals. A lot of people skip this important stage. They get motivated, and then they want to skip right to the action stage. But there is so much value in preparation! You can't go from sitting on the couch to deciding the next day you want to run a marathon. You've got to plan, prepare, and train. This is what the preparation stage is all about. If you want to change something, you've got to have a plan.

Stage 4: Action—This is the stage most people think about when it comes to change because it's the stage where you can actually see change happen. This is the stage where you start hitting the gym, showing up to your counseling sessions, attending that AA meeting, or getting some accountability in your life. You start intentionally doing things differently instead of defaulting to what you've always done.

Remember how we talked about the fact that healing is not linear? Well, this is when you'll really see that come into play. Sometimes, you'll be in the action phase for a stage and then find yourself back in preparation mode, or even all the way back in contemplation or precontemplation. Maybe you failed at something, relapsed, or struggled again. Now you've got to get motivation back, tweak your plan, get better support, get back up, and try again. Because eventually, as long as you don't give up, the action stage will lead you to the next stage of healing.

Stage 5: Maintenance—The last stage of healing is what it looks like to live changed because eventually long-term actions lead to long-term habits. You've made progress and moved to a new place. You've worked through your trauma, found freedom from panic attacks, overcome your demons, said goodbye to that addiction, and reached the goals you were hoping to achieve. This doesn't mean you'll never struggle again. In fact, maybe you'll always walk with a little bit of a limp in these areas. But you'll continue to push through, fight back, and get back up when you've been knocked down because if you've done it once, you can do it again.

Your Turn

What about you? When it comes to things that need to change, areas that need to mature, places you need to grow—where do you fall on the stages of change? I don't want to leave you with just perspective, I want to leave you with a plan. I want to leave you with the hope and courage to take the next steps. It's easy to dream of where we want to be, but what sets healthy people apart from unhealthy people comes down to the steps they make to move toward change. Take some time to copy the stages below into your journal, and answer the questions that go with them:

Precontemplation: Write one specific area in your life that you want to see changed.

Contemplation: Write a list of reasons WHY this needs to change, and consider also writing a mission statement or a theme verse from Scripture to help you remember why you're choosing to change.

Preparation: Write three things you can do that will motivate and prepare you to move in the direction of change in this area of your life.

> You can either check out or you can change.

Action: Write three practical action steps you will do regularly or even daily to move you in the direction of healing and change.

Maintenance: Take a moment to imagine what it will feel like to achieve change in this area, and write out your feelings and reactions to that change.

One year from today will be here before you know it. And you can either stay the same, or you can get better, healthier, stronger. You can either check out, or you can change.

How Are You, *Really*?

I don't know who you are, what you've been through, or where you are today. I don't know your story, your struggles, or your pain. But if you were sitting in front of me today, I'd look you straight in the eyes and ask you this question: "Are you *really* okay?" I'm not looking for a pat answer. It's easy to say we're okay without really thinking about it. But I want to dig deeper than that. I want to push harder than that.

How are you doing in your life right here and right now?

What are the problem spots you're seeing in your personal life and in your relationships?

What are the feelings you're facing deep down inside?

What wounds are you carrying, and how are you dealing with them?

Have you taken the time to ask the hard questions and get the hard answers?

Are you living intentionally toward emotional, spiritual, mental, and physical health?

Are you moving toward becoming healthy, or are you staying the same?

What concerns me the most are not the people who see their need for change, but the people that don't. Don't ever fool yourself into thinking that somehow being a Christian means you have arrived. Just because you're a Christian doesn't mean you're healthy. Your soul is secure, but your sanctification is on ongoing process.

> Just because you're a Christian doesn't mean you're healthy.

Working out your faith requires work, energy, and intention (Philippians 2:12). But if you're willing, God is waiting. Waiting to give you the strength that you need to say no to the old and put on the new (2 Corinthians 5:17). Waiting to help you heal from your hurts (Isaiah 53:5). Waiting to empower you and equip you (Isaiah 41:10). Waiting to strengthen you and protect you (2 Thessalonians 3:3). Waiting to give you exactly what you need for today (2 Peter 1:3). Waiting to show you that you can do all things by His strength (Philippians 4:13). I'm believing that for you and praying it over you. It's time to be intentional. It's time to get healthy. It's time to ask the hard questions and come face-to-face with the real answer: Are you *really* okay?

Journaling Questions: 5-Minute Final Checkup

- As you reflect on the four areas of health: emotional, spiritual, mental, and physical, which area do you feel led to focus on first and why?

- As you think through that specific area of your life, take a few moments to complete the stages of change activity above, focusing on one specific thing in which you would like to begin the process of change.

- In the past, what have been some barriers that have prevented you from moving toward healing?

- The message of TrueLoveDates.com is that "healthy people make healthy relationships." How has your level of overall health impacted your closest relationships?

- Consider partnering with a licensed professional counselor as you begin this important journey of living intentionally toward emotional, spiritual, mental, and physical health.

ACKNOWLEDGMENTS

There's so much gratitude in my heart as I release this book into the world that it's hard to know where to begin.

First and foremost, *I'm grateful to my Jesus* for the promise, even while I was in the pit of darkness and depression, that He would use the broken and shattered pieces of my heart to bring healing to many. This book is an offering to You, Lord, and I trust wholeheartedly that You will send it exactly where it needs to go. Thank You for allowing me to be used in this way. What a privilege.

To my husband John, the past 13 years of our marriage I have watched you step up in so many ways. But the one thing I am most grateful for is how you have learned to walk by my side through the struggles of depression and anxiety. You've been my steady rock, my sounding board, my prayer warrior, and my best friend. You've held my arms up when I was too weak to hold them up for myself. Thank you for your constant and steady love, and for always seeing the best in me. I couldn't do any of this without you.

To Dr. Steven Hamon, my dear friend, colleague, and mentor. So much of who I am as a counselor is because of what you have poured into my life over the years. Thank you for coming alongside of me when I was at my weakest and reminding me of who I am and what God has called me to do. Your impact on my life cannot be measured.

To Levi Lusko, thank you for your heart and support for this message of health and healing. You're a pastor who not only preaches this message but lives it out on the daily. I've witnessed that with my own eyes and I'm grateful for your leadership and example. Thank you for the words you wrote in this foreword, but more so, thank you for walking the talk.

To my Harvest House family, never has there been a publishing company that has truly felt like family. Kathleen—thank you for praying with me, celebrating with me, and mourning with me through hard times. You're more than an editor, you're a friend. Sherrie—thank you for being not only the best leader, but truly the best *cheer*leader. Your encouragement and support stand out like a shining light. To every single person on the team of bringing this message into the world: thank you for your hard work and dedication to this project.

To my little people, you kids keep me grounded like nothing else can. I love each of you so much and I pray that as you read these words one day, you'll be brave enough to ask the hard questions and invite the Lord to heal every single part of your life. Thank you for all the title ideas, illustration suggestions, and serious distractions along the way. You guys are my primary ministry, and I'm honored to be able to call myself your mom!

And to each and every person reading this book, getting ready to answer the question: *Are you really ok?* Thank you for your bravery. I believe the Lord is going to bring healing and hope as we embark on this journey together.

ABOUT THE AUTHOR

DEBRA FILETA is a licensed professional counselor, national speaker, relationship expert, and author of *Choosing Marriage, True Love Dates,* and *Love in Every Season.* She's also the host of the hotline style podcast, *Love + Relationships with Debra Fileta.* Her popular relationship advice blog, *TrueLoveDates.com,* reaches millions of people with the message of healthy relationships.

Debra and her husband, John, have been happily married for more than a decade and live in Lancaster, Pennsylvania, with their beautiful children. Connect with her on Facebook or Instagram (@True LoveDates), or book a speaking engagement or online session with her today at TrueLoveDates.com.

NOTES

Introduction: You're Not as Healthy as You Think You Are

1. Mark D. Alicke and Olesya Govorun, "The Better-than-Average Effect," *The Self in Social Judgment* (New York: Psychology Press, 2005), 83-106.

2. Rosie Meek, Mark D. Alicke, and Sarah Taylor, "Behind Bars but Above the Bar: Prisoners Consider Themselves More Prosocial than Non-Prisoners," *British Journal of Social Psychology* 53, no. 2 (June 2014): 396-403, doi: 10.1111/bjso.12060.

Chapter 1—Going Underneath the Surface: Emotional Awareness

1. Robert Evans, "Blast From the Past," *SmithsonianMag.com*, July 2002, www.smithsonianmag .com/history/blast-from-the-past-65102374.

2. Ibid.

3. Robert Plutchik, *The Emotions* (Lanham, MD: University Press of America, 1991).

4. K.S. Kassam and W.B. Mendes, "The Effects of Measuring Emotion: Physiological Reactions to Emotional Situations Depend on Whether Someone Is Asking," *PLoS One* 8, no. 7 (June 5, 2013): doi: 10.1371/journal.pone.0064959.

5. Paul Ekman, "What Is Sadness?" Paul Ekman Group, www.paulekman.com/universal emotions/what-is-sadness.

6. T.H. Holmes and R.H. Rahe, "The Social Readjustment Rating Scale," *Journal of Psychosomatic Research* 11, no. 2 (August 1967): 213-18, doi: 10.1016/0022-3999(67)90010-4.

7. Tommy Nelson and Steve Leavitt, *Walking on Water When You Feel Like You're Drowning: Finding Hope in Life's Darkest Moments* (Carol Stream, IL: Tyndale House, 2012).

Chapter 2—Patterns Lead to Process: Emotional History

1. Judith Ouellette and Wendy Wood, "Habit and Intention in Everyday Life: The Multiple Processes by Which Past Behavior Predicts Future Behavior," *Psychological Bulletin* 124, no. 1 (July 1998): 54-74, doi: 10.1037/0033-2909.124.1.54.

2. Ibid., 54.

3. Hank Hanegraaff, "Are Generational Curses Biblical?" Christianity.com, accessed June 6, 2020, www.christianity.com/blogs/hank-hanegraaff/are-generational-curses-biblical.html.

4. Shaun King, "Stressed Out Pastors, Crazy Sins, and the Death of Pastor Zach Tims," Church Leaders.com, August 23, 2011, www.churchleaders.com/pastors/pastor-blogs/153724-shaun_ king_stressed_out_pastors_crazy_sins_and_the_death_of_pastor_zach_tims.html.

5. Dima Mazen Qato, Katharine Ozenberger, and Mark Olfson, "Prevalence of Prescription Medications with Depression as a Potential Adverse Effect Among Adults in the United States," *JAMA* 319, no. 22 (June 2018): 2289-98, doi: 10.1001/jama.2018.6741.

6. Monique Tello, "Depression: Common Medication Side Effect?" *Harvard Health Publishing*, July 16, 2018, www.health.harvard.edu/blog/depression-common-medication-side-effect-2018071614259.

Chapter 3—God Is More Real than My Reality: Emotional Control

1. Laurie Kelly McCorry, "Physiology of the Autonomic Nervous System," *American Journal of Pharmaceutical Education* 71, no. 4 (August 2007): 78, www.ncbi.nlm.nih.gov/pmc/articles/PMC1959222.

2. Bill Gaultier, "Jesus Is a Feeler with 39 Emotions," SoulShepherding.org, accessed June 8, 2020, www.soulshepherding.org/jesus-is-a-feeler-with-39-emotions.

3. "What Is Hematidrosis?" WebMd.com, accessed June 8, 2020, www.webmd.com/a-to-z-guides/hematidrosis-hematohidrosis#1.

4. Ewa Kacewicz, Richard Slatcher, and James Pennebaker, "Expressive Writing: An Alternative to Traditional Methods," *Low-Cost Approaches to Promote Physical and Mental Health* (New York: Springer, 2007), 271-84, doi: 10.1007/0-387-36899-X_13.

5. Ibid.

Chapter 5—Hello, My Name Is _____: My View of Self

1. David Veale, Lucinda Gledhill, Polyxeni Christodoulou, and John Hodsoll, "Body Dysmorphic Disorder in Different Settings: A Systematic Review and Estimated Weighted Prevalence," *Body Image* 18 (September 2016): 168-86, doi: 10.1016/j.bodyim.2016.07.003.

2. David Mataix-Cols et al., "A Pilot Randomized Controlled Trial of Cognitive Behavioral Therapy for Adolescents with Body Dysmorphic Disorder," *Journal of the American Academy of Child & Adolescent Psychiatry* 54, no. 11 (November 1, 2015): 895-904, doi: 10.1016/j.jaac.2015.08.011.

3. Debra Fileta, *True Love Dates: Your Indispensable Guide to Finding the Love of Your Life* (Grand Rapids, MI: Zondervan, 2013).

Chapter 6—Significant Others: My View of Relationships

1. Wess Stafford, "'Just a Minute' Wess Stafford Part 1," 100 Huntley Street, July 25, 2012, YouTube video, www.youtube.com/watch?v=4Bi8UDA5kb4.

Chapter 7—What's on Repeat? Cognitive Distortions

1. Catherine Pittman and Elizabeth Karle, *Rewire Your Anxious Brain: How to Use the Neuroscience of Fear to End Anxiety, Panic, and Worry* (Oakland, CA: New Harbinger Publications, 2015), 6.

2. Ibid.

Chapter 8—Anxiety, Depression, and the Church: Mental Health Matters

1. Heather Vacek, *Madness: American Protestant Responses to Mental Illness* (Waco, TX: Baylor University Press, 2015).

2. Catherine Pittman and Elizabeth Karle, *Rewire Your Anxious Brain: How to Use the Neuroscience of Fear to End Anxiety, Panic, and Worry* (Oakland, CA: New Harbinger Publications, 2015), 27.

3. Ibid., 29.

4. Ibid., 30.

5. Pirjo Kinnunen, Eila Laukkanen, and Jari Kylmä, "Associations Between Psychosomatic Symptoms in Adolescence and Mental Health Symptoms in Early Adulthood," *International Journal of Nursing Practice* 16, no. 1 (February 2010): 43-50, doi: 10.1111/j.1440-172X.2009.01782.x.

6. Gerd Karin Natvig, Grethe Albrektsen, and Ulla Qvarnstrøm, "Psychosomatic Symptoms Among Victims of School Bullying," *Journal of Health Psychology* 6, no. 4 (July 1, 2001): 365-77, doi: 10.1177/135910530100600401.

7. K. Kroenke and A.D. Mangelsdorff, "Common Symptoms in Ambulatory Care: Incidence, Evaluation, Therapy, and Outcome," *The American Journal of Medicine* 86, no. 3 (March 1989): 262-66, doi: 10.1016/0002-9343(89)90293-3.

8. Arthur J. Barsky, E. John Orav, and David W. Bates, "Somatization Increases Medical Utilization and Costs Independent of Psychiatric and Medical Comorbidity," *Archives of General Psychiatry* 62, no. 8 (August 2005): 903-10, doi: 10.1001/archpsyc.62.8.903.

9. David O. Antonuccio, William G. Danton, and Garland Y. DeNelsky, "Psychotherapy Versus Medication for Depression: Challenging the Conventional Wisdom with Data," *Professional Psychology: Research and Practice* 26, no. 6 (1995): 574-85, doi: 10.1037/0735-7028.26.6.574.

10. Pim Cuijpers, "Four Decades of Outcome Research on Psychotherapies for Adult Depression: An Overview of a Series of Meta-Analyses," *Canadian Psychology* 58, no. 1 (2017): 7-19, doi: 10.1037/cap0000096.

11. Ibid.

Chapter 9—Trauma Messes with Your Head: Peeling Back the Layers

1. Carolyn Weber, *Holy Is the Day: Living in the Gift of the Present* (Downers Grove, IL: InterVarsity Press, 2013), 39.

2. Catherine Pittman and Elizabeth Karle, *Rewire Your Anxious Brain: How to Use the Neuroscience of Fear to End Anxiety, Panic, and Worry* (Oakland, CA: New Harbinger Publications, 2015), 41-42.

3. J.I. Packer, *Knowing God* (Downers Grove, IL: InterVarsity Press, 2001), 23.

4. Victoria Follette, Kathleen M. Palm, and Adria N. Pearson, "Mindfulness and Trauma: Implications for treatment," *Journal of Rational-Emotive & Cognitive-Behavior Therapy* 24, no. 1 (Spring 2006): 45-61, doi: 10.1007/s10942-006-0025-2.

5. Maria Karekla, John P. Forsyth, and Megan M. Kelly, "Emotional Avoidance and Panicogenic Responding to a Biological Challenge Procedure," *Behavior Therapy* 35, no. 4 (Autumn 2004): 725-46, doi: 10.1016/S0005-7894(04)80017-0.

6. Follette et al., "Mindfulness and Trauma."

7. Charles Stone, *Holy Noticing: The Bible, Your Brain, and the Mindful Space Between Moments* (Chicago, IL: Moody Publishers, 2019), 34.

8. Ibid., 94.

9. As an additional resource, visit Abide.co. This is an app for guided Christian meditation.

Chapter 10—Back to the Basics: The Body-Mind Connection

1. Jill Littrell, "The Mind-Body Connection: Not Just a Theory Anymore," *Social Work in Health Care* 46, no. 4 (2008): 17-37, doi: 10.1300/j010v46n04_02.

2. Franklin C. Brown, Walter C. Buboltz Jr., and Barlow Soper, "Relationship of Sleep Hygiene Awareness, Sleep Hygiene Practices, and Sleep Quality in University Students," *Behavioral Medicine* 28, no. 1 (2002): 33-38, doi: 10.1080/08964280209596396.

3. Zohreh Yazdi, Ziba Loukzadeh, Parichehr Moghaddam, and Shabnam Jalilolghadr, "Sleep Hygiene Practices and Their Relation to Sleep Quality in Medical Students of Qazvin University of Medical Sciences," *Journal of Caring Sciences* 5, no. 2 (2016): 153-60, doi: 10.15171/jcs.2016.016.

4. Ibid.

5. M. Basil Pennington, *Centering Prayer: Renewing Ancient Christian Prayer Form* (Garden City, NY: Doubleday, 1980), 68-69.

6. Lynette L. Craft, and Frank M. Perna, "The Benefits of Exercise for the Clinically Depressed," *The Primary Care Companion to the Journal of Clinical Psychiatry* 6, no. 3 (2004): 104-11, doi: 10.4088/pcc.v06n0301.

7. Laura Lachance and Drew Ramsey, "Food, Mood, and Brain Health: Implications for the Modern Clinician," *Missouri Medicine* 112, no. 2 (March–April 2015): 111-15, www.ncbi.nlm.nih.gov/pmc/articles/PMC6170050/.

8. Roger A.H. Adan et al., "Nutritional Psychiatry: Towards Improving Mental Health by What You Eat," *European Neuropsychopharmacology* 29, no. 12 (December 2019): 1321-32, doi: 10.1016/j.euroneuro.2019.10.011.

9. Lachance and Ramsey, "Food, Mood, and Brain Health."

10. J. Rienks, A.J. Dobson, and G.D. Mishra, "Mediterranean Dietary Pattern and Prevalence and Incidence of Depressive Symptoms in Mid-Aged Women: Results from a Large Community-Based Prospective Study," *European Journal of Clinical Nutrition* 67, no. 1 (January 2013): 75-82, doi: 10.1038/ejcn.2012.193.

Chapter 12—Time Doesn't Heal All Wounds: One Year from Today

1. Jon Courson, "Limping Through Life," Calvary Chapel of Philadelphia, https://www.ccphilly.org/limping-through-life/.

An Invitation to Love Well Through the Four Seasons

Every relationship goes through four life-changing seasons that play a pivotal role in taking your relationship to the next level. But depending on how you navigate each season, your relationship will either strengthen and grow, or it will slowly begin to fade.

- Maybe your relationship is in the first blooms of spring, when friendship takes root and attraction blossoms.

- Maybe you're in the season of summer, and things are starting to heat up–spiritually, emotionally, and physically.

- Maybe you're deep in fall, and your true colors are starting to shine through.

- Or maybe you're in winter, when the passion cools down and it would be all too easy to let the relationship freeze over.

Whether you're single, dating, engaged, or married, join author, counselor, and relationship expert Debra Fileta, creator of TrueLoveDates .com, as she takes you on an eye-opening psychological and spiritual journey through the four seasons of every healthy relationship. You'll learn to...

Recognize each season as it comes and navigate it with intention, focus, and practical steps.

Avoid the pitfalls of each stage by preparing for the hard moments and seeing them as opportunities to grow and connect.

Celebrate not just the magical moments of each season, but the day-to-day choices that pave the way for a lasting relationship.

Is Marriage
Worth it?

Many couples say "I do" with a combination of high hopes and fairy tale fantasies—but there's a difference between the *expectations* of marriage and its *reality*. Whether you're married, single, or dating, now is the time to ask yourself: *What steps can I take today to build an incredible marriage for tomorrow?*

With compassion and clarity, licensed counselor and relationship expert Debra Fileta shows that when we can work through the struggles of marriage, we get to experience the joys! Learn about eight powerful choices that will encourage and equip you to take your marriage from *average* to *exceptional* and find astonishing survey results from thousands of singles and couples on topics like love and attraction, sex, conflict, and communication.

A beautiful exchange occurs when you learn what it means to choose *we* before *me*. Discover practical steps that will give you confidence and courage on the adventure of *Choosing Marriage*.

To learn more about Harvest House books and
to read sample chapters, visit our website:

www.harvesthousepublishers.com

HARVEST HOUSE PUBLISHERS
EUGENE, OREGON